RED CHRIST

The Tatsinskaya Airfield Raid 1942

ROBERT FORCZYK

First published in Great Britain in 2012 by Osprey Publishing,
Midland House, West Way, Botley, Oxford, OX2 0PH, UK
44-02 23rd St, Suite 219, Long Island City, NY 11101, USA

Osprey Publishing is part of the Osprey Group

E-mail: info@ospreypublishing.com

A CIP catalogue record for this book is available from the British Library

Print ISBN: 978 1 84908 586 1
PDF e-book ISBN: 978 1 84908 587 8
EPUB e-book ISBN: 978 1 78096 406 5

Page layout by Bounford.com
Index by Sandra Shotter
Typeset in Sabon
Maps by Bounford.com
Originated by United Graphics Pte., Singapore
Printed in China through Worldprint Ltd.

12 13 14 15 16 10 9 8 7 6 5 4 3 2 1

Osprey Publishing is supporting the Woodland Trust, the UK's leading woodland conservation charity, by funding the dedication of trees.

www.ospreypublishing.com

CONTENTS

INTRODUCTION

At 1400hrs on 23 November 1942, Soviet troops from the 4th Mechanized Corps linked up with troops from the 4th Tank Corps near Kalach, completing the encirclement of Generalfeldmarschall Friedrich von Paulus' 6. Armee within the Stalingrad pocket. In just four days, the Soviet winter counter-offensive known as Operation *Uranus* had succeeded in reversing the Red Army's desperate situation at Stalingrad and seizing the strategic initiative from the Wehrmacht. Inside the Stalingrad pocket, the trapped Axis force consisted of the 6. Armee, IV Armeekorps from 4. Panzerarmee and the remnants of the Romanian 4th Army, with a total of 256,000 German and 11,000 Romanian soldiers. The completion of the Soviet encirclement of Armeeoberkommando 6 (6th Army High Command; AOK 6) was an unprecedented catastrophe for Hitler's Third Reich and the culmination of a decade of doctrinal development and experimentation in mechanized warfare by the Red Army.

Yet Hitler was resolved to save the trapped forces in Stalingrad, and immediately decided upon three counter-measures to mitigate the Soviet success. Firstly, he ordered the Luftwaffe to mount an airlift from a number of airfields outside the pocket in order to sustain the trapped forces. Secondly, he authorized the formation of Heeresgruppe Don (Army Group Don) under one of his most brilliant commanders, Generalfeldmarschall Erich von Manstein, and tasked him to establish a new front on the Chir River with those forces not trapped inside Stalingrad. This new front line, built mostly out of extemporized units and the remnants of the Romanian divisions shattered by Operation *Uranus*, would provide the springboard for a relief operation known as *Wintergewitter*, which would be mounted in order to re-establish a ground link to AOK 6. Third, Hitler ordered the rapid transfer of significant reinforcements to von Manstein's Heeresgruppe Don in order for him to be able to launch *Wintergewitter* within about two to three weeks. These reinforcements included the 6., 11., 17. and 23. Panzer-Divisionen. Hitler determined that with a bit of luck and determination, the Soviet ring around Stalingrad could be broken and the whole affair reduced to a temporary setback for the German conquest of the Soviet Union.

23 NOVEMBER 1942

1400hrs Encirclement of Stalingrad complete

VASILY M. BADANOV (1895–1971)

After spending two years in a teacher's seminary, Badanov enlisted in the Russian Imperial Army in 1915 and served in World War I. He distinguished himself in combat and quickly rose to command an infantry company. By 1916, Badanov received a commission as a reserve officer, but when the Russian Revolution erupted a year later, he was elected as people's representative for his regimental committee. Soon thereafter, Badanov joined the Red Army and served both as a commissar and a staff officer in the campaign against Admiral Kolchak's White forces in the Urals in 1919.

After the Russian Civil War, Badanov transferred to the OGPU secret police for nearly six years, and commanded a regiment in one of its divisions. (The OGPU was involved in suppressing internal political dissent and was responsible for the creation of the Gulag prison system.) In 1927, Badanov returned to the Red Army and went through a series of training assignments that eventually landed him a role as an instructor at Saratov in 1930, where the first Red Army tank school was forming. Badanov transferred to the new tank branch and was closely involved in the Red Army's tank training programme of the 1930s. In 1937, he was commander of the Poltava Automobile Technical College, where tank maintenance was taught. Badanov managed to avoid the purges – his OGPU connections may have helped – and as war approached he sought to get a combat command.

At the start of the German invasion in June 1941, Badanov was assigned command of the 55th Tank Division in the 21st Army during the battle of Smolensk. However, this poorly equipped division had only a short combat career before it was disbanded due to heavy losses. In August 1941, Badanov was given command of the 12th Tank Brigade, one of the new tank units, equipped with KV, T-34 and T-70 tanks, and which served with the Southwest Front.

On 19 April 1942, Badanov took command of the newly formed 24th Tank Corps and spent the next few months preparing the formation for combat. Although Badanov accomplished his mission during the Tatsinskaya raid, and was awarded the Order of Suvorov 2nd degree for doing so, he apparently angered Stalin by retreating without authorization. Consequently, Badanov never received the Hero of the Soviet Union (HSU) award.

He remained in command of the renamed 2nd Guards Tank Corps until June 1943, when he took command of the 4th Tank Army. This formation was vastly larger than his previous command and had 37,000 troops and 652 tanks when it participated in Operation *Kutuzov*, the Soviet counter-offensive to retake the Orel salient in July 1943. Unlike the Tatsinskaya raid, Badanov's tank army had to push forward against stiff German resistance and it suffered heavy losses. Badanov later led the 4th Tank Army during the Lvov–Sandomierz offensive in March 1944, until he was seriously wounded. After recovering from concussion, he spent the next two years in high-level training assignments.

Following the war, he commanded Soviet tank and mechanized forces in East Germany in 1946–1950 and retired in 1953. He later wrote his account of the Tatsinskaya raid in 1968, but it was typical of the politically influenced history produced in the Soviet era and was riddled with numerous errors and omissions.

Ju-52 transports en route to deliver supplies to the encircled 6. Armee in Stalingrad, December 1942. The Luftwaffe was obliged to cobble together a large-scale aerial resupply operation in a matter of days under the worst weather conditions possible. (Author)

On 24 November 1942 – the day after the Soviet link-up near Kalach – Generaloberst Wolfram von Richtofen's Luftflotte 4 (4th Air Fleet) began an airlift to sustain AOK 6 in Stalingrad. Von Richtofen hastily assembled a force of transports and bombers at Tatsinskaya and Morozovskaya airfields to conduct the resupply operation. Although the Luftwaffe had only sufficient aircraft on hand to provide roughly one-eighth of the AOK 6 daily supply requirements, it had gained plenty of experience with aerial resupply operations in Russia during the first winter of the war on the Eastern Front. During February–April 1942, the Luftwaffe had successfully supplied nearly 100,000 German troops in the Demyansk and Kholm pockets for more than two months, until a ground relief operation succeeded in reaching them. Reichsmarschall Hermann Göring – ignoring the effects of harsh winter weather and the larger scale required to keep open an aerial bridge to Stalingrad – assured Hitler that his Luftwaffe could sustain AOK 6 until a relief operation was launched. However, it would take several weeks for Manstein to gather his forces for *Wintergewitter* and, in the meantime, it was up to Luftflotte 4 to keep AOK 6 from crumbling.

On 30 November, Generalleutnant Martin Fiebig, the commander of VIII Fliegerkorps (VIII Air Corps), was made *Luftversorgungsführer* (air resupply leader) and he established his headquarters at Tatsinskaya airfield. The Germans had first occupied Tatsinskaya on 21 July and had begun improving the base even before Operation *Uranus* had created the necessity for an airlift operation. Although the 1,500m (5,000ft)-long grass runway was adequate under normal weather conditions, keeping the field clear of deep snow once winter arrived was a gargantuan and manpower-intensive task. It was also extremely difficult to keep aircraft operational in sub-zero temperatures, and required specialized warming trucks to pre-heat aircraft engines. Given the difficulty of keeping just these two primary airfields operational, Fiebig decided to concentrate all the available Ju-52 transport groups at Tatsinskaya and put them under the command of Oberst Hans Förster, while the He-111 and other bomber units pressed into service as transports were based at Morozovskaya. This was a risky but sensible decision, since it simplified logistical and maintenance support. Both airfields were located adjacent to the main east–west rail line supporting Heeresgruppe Don and supplies of fuel and ammunition could easily be trans-loaded from trains to the nearby airfields. When Fiebig made this decision in late November 1942, the nearest Soviet troops were more than 80km (50 miles) away from either airfield, so ground defence did not seem a priority. Heeresgruppe Don had formed Armee Abteilung Hollidt (Army Detachment Hollidt) to hold the area between the Chir and Don rivers, and although this sector was thinly manned there did not appear to be an immediate threat to the airfields.

The airlift got off to a shaky start and never came close to meeting AOK 6's supply needs, but it did succeed in evacuating thousands of casualties from inside the pocket and providing a morsel of hope that somehow catastrophe could be avoided. Manstein gave Generaloberst Hermann Hoth responsibility for conducting *Wintergewitter*, but the promised reinforcements arrived more slowly than expected and only the 6. and 23. Panzer-Divisionen were available by the second week of December. Soviet attacks against Armee Abteilung Hollidt forced Manstein to keep 11. Panzer-Division to hold the Chir front. Nevertheless, Manstein recognized that he could no longer delay the relief operation if there was to be any chance of

Hoth's Panzers advance towards Stalingrad across the steppe during Operation *Wintergewitter*, the attempt to relieve 6. Armee in mid-December 1942. It was a critical requirement that the airlift kept 6. Armee in fighting condition so it could break out to meet Hoth's rescue force when the time came. (Nik Cornish, WH 683)

24 NOVEMBER 1942

Airlift operations to sustain forces in Stalingrad commence

success and he was forced to begin *Wintergewitter* with the forces on hand. On 12 December, 151km (94 miles) southeast of Tatsinskaya, Hoth attacked with the two Panzer divisions of LVII Panzerkorps and initially made rapid progress towards Stalingrad. For a few days, it even seemed that Hoth might pull off a miracle and rescue at least some of the trapped AOK 6.

Unfortunately for the Wehrmacht, Operation *Uranus* was only the opening round in the Red Army's winter counter-offensive in southern Russia. The Stavka had no intention of allowing either *Wintergewitter* or the Luftwaffe airlift to de-rail their plans for crushing the Stalingrad pocket and then driving on to Rostov. Four days after Manstein began *Wintergewitter*, General-leytenant (Lieutenant-General) Nikolai Vatutin's Southwest Front began Operation *Little Saturn* against the Italian VIII Army on Heeresgruppe Don's left flank. Spearheading Vatutin's offensive, the 1st Guards Army and 3rd Guards Army committed three tank corps, one mechanized corps and nine rifle divisions against the thinly spread Italian forces and were able to achieve a number of breakthroughs by the second day of the offensive. Two tank corps – the 24th Tank Corps under General-major (Major-General) Vasily M. Badanov and the 25th Tank Corps under Major-General Petr P. Pavlov – were initially held in reserve. Once the Italian front was broken, Badanov and Pavlov were ordered to advance into the breach and to operate as independent mobile groups to strike deep behind enemy lines. Their objectives were the Luftwaffe airfields at Tatsinskaya and Morozovskaya, located 232km (144 miles) to the south.

ORIGINS

> We are at the dawn of a new epoch in military art, and must move from a linear strategy to a deep strategy.
>
> – Georgy Isserson, Frunze Military Academy, 1933

Once the Red Army began to settle into the habits of a professional military force after the conclusion of the Russian Civil War, one of the first questions that its leadership began to address was what kind of forces it would need for future military operations. The Russian Army had always been offensively oriented. The Red Army adopted this ethos as well, but recognized that standard linear offensive methods had not worked well against the defence-in-depth tactics that appeared during World War I. Particularly vexing questions were how best to break a prepared enemy defence – which had been achieved on occasion in 1914–18 – and how to convert a breakthrough from a local tactical victory into a wider success that yielded decisive results.

Despite its many horrific consequences, the Revolution enabled a new cadre of revisionist Russian military thinkers to come into their own, and by the late 1920s they were proposing a radical re-think of Soviet military doctrine. These revisionists recognized that the Red Army needed more than just large infantry armies, and they aggressively advocated new tactics based upon tanks, mobile artillery and close air support. In 1929, Lieutenant-General Vladimir K. Triandafillov wrote *The Character of Operations of Modern Armies*, which first began to establish the concepts of *glubokiy boy* (Deep Battle) and advocated the formation of large tank units. Triandafillov also conceived of the breakthrough being achieved by a *udarnaia armiia* (shock army), consisting of up to 15 rifle divisions, reinforced with heavy artillery and tanks. Mikhail Tukhachevsky also contributed to the early development of Deep Battle theory and the promotion of mechanization in the Red Army.

Initially, Deep Battle was conceived as merely a tactical solution to breaking through a World War I-style defence, by coordinating artillery,

24 NOV–2 DEC 1942

Operation *Saturn* plan is developed

tanks and airpower to achieve a powerful combat synergy, but initially the depth of penetration was envisioned to be only about 15km (9 miles). The Red Army formed its first experimental tank brigade in May 1930, and two years later the Soviets established two mechanized corps, each with 463 light tanks. However, the Red Army was uncertain about the best way to use tanks on the battlefield – a debate that was also occurring in other major armies.

Eventually, three distinct doctrinal approaches emerged within the Red Army and shaped the development of its armoured forces used in World War II. Foremost was the direct infantry support role, designated as the primary function of NPP tanks, which resulted in the T-26 series light tanks. Yet it was recognized that these light tanks were not powerful enough to break through a dense fortified zone, so DPP tanks were conceived as heavy infantry support armour and resulted in the T-28 and T-35, and later the KV-1 series. Finally, once a breakthrough was achieved, the exploitation phase would be conducted with cavalry and DD tanks, which had the range and mobility to operate well beyond the initial front line. At first, the Red Army built the BT series fast tanks to fulfil the DD mission, but rapid technological progress enabled the development of the far superior T-34 tank just before the outbreak of World War II. An important point here is that unlike the German tank developers, Soviet military leaders ensured that the DD tanks they built had the range, reliability and mobility to conduct far-ranging operations. In this case, doctrine shaped weapons development – as it should – and the Soviet Union perfected a reliable and powerful diesel tank engine that it would use to power its BT-7M and T-34 tanks. Consequently, the best Soviet tanks at the start of World War II had double the operational range of standard British, French and German armour.

As the Red Army began to field its first large armoured units, its doctrine continued to evolve from the tactical issues of Deep Battle into the wider

Soviet BT-7 tanks on display during the May Day parade. The Red Army quickly seized upon mechanized warfare during the inter-war period and formed its first mechanized corps in 1932. BT-series tanks and the next-generation T-34 tank were designed for speed and manoeuvrability specifically for mechanized exploitation operations. (Nik Cornish, RA 76)

concept of *glubokaya operatsiya* (Deep Operations). Although Triandafillov died in 1931, a brilliant military theoretician was soon to follow in his footsteps and expand his concepts into a workable military doctrine. In 1932, Kombrig (Brigade Commander) Georgy Isserson, an instructor at the Frunze Military Academy, wrote *The Evolution of Operational Art*, followed the next year by *The Fundamentals of the Deep Operation*. Isserson took some of Triandafillov's basic ideas on Deep Battle but developed a sophisticated doctrine of how the Red Army could break an enemy's defences in greater depth. Whereas Triandafillov discussed offensive penetrations to a depth of 15–20km (9–12 miles), Isserson boldly envisioned penetrations of up to 200km (124 miles). Isserson accepted the concept of the initial breakthrough by a reinforced shock army, but was far more interested in what came next. He recommended that after a breach in the enemy's lines was achieved, a mechanized corps, possibly reinforced with a cavalry corps, should spearhead the exploitation phase in conjunction with landings of paratroopers behind enemy lines and air interdiction missions to prevent enemy reserves from interfering. Isserson dubbed this mechanized force as an *echelon razvitiia uspekha* (success development echelon; ERU), and claimed that it could penetrate up to 150–200km (93–124 miles) behind the initial enemy lines in a matter of three days. He wrote that the ERU should raid deep into the enemy's rear areas, overrunning airfields, railroad stations and logistics bases in order to de-stabilize the enemy defence across a broad area. Yet Isserson cautioned that the ERU should return to friendly lines within three days, or it ran the risk of becoming isolated and destroyed by the enemy's mobile reserves. Written in 1933, this description of the ERU's mission proved to be an astonishingly accurate foretaste of the 1942 Tatsinskaya raid.

Tukhachevsky accepted Isserson's theories and classified *The Fundamentals of the Deep Operation* as 'Top Secret'. He then codified Triandafillov's and Isserson's theories in 1935 as *Instructions on Deep Battle*. The Red Army High Command decided to test this new doctrine with the 35th Mechanized Corps during the Kiev Military District (MD) summer manoeuvres, and the results were promising. In 1936, the experiment was repeated in the Byelorussian MD manoeuvres, which added paratroopers into the scenario. As a result of the theoretical and practical testing, the Red Army issued its Field Service Regulations for 1936 (PU-36), which fully endorsed mechanized warfare and Deep Operations as official doctrine. Although the Red Army leadership was uncertain how far a mechanized corps (re-named as tank corps in August 1938) could operate behind enemy lines, they recognized that decisive results could be achieved rapidly if a large tank unit could reach and sever an enemy's lines of communications.

Just as the Red Army reached the cusp of modern military theory, Josef Stalin and his cronies decided that Tukhachevsky and his disciples were using mechanization as a means to reduce the Communist Party's control over the Red Army. He began a purge in June 1937 that resulted in the execution of Tukhachevsky and other mechanization advocates. Isserson survived the initial purge, but was arrested in June 1941 and spent the entire war in a

Brigade Commander Georgy S. Isserson (1898–1976), an instructor at the Frunze Military Academy and then a member of the Red Army's General Staff. He was one of the most significant prophets of the theory of Deep Operations and he also developed the doctrine for using mechanized corps to conduct raids behind the enemy's front lines to attack their airfields and lines of communication. (Russian State Military Archives)

labour camp in Kazakhstan. Once the advocates of modernization were removed or silenced, the Red Army abandoned the Deep Operations doctrine and a coterie of reactionary generals argued that deep armoured exploitation operations were actually not feasible. In November 1939, the tank corps were disbanded and their tanks relegated to brigade-size units intended purely for infantry support. Yet the stunning success of German Panzer units in the opening campaigns in Poland and France forced even Stalin and the most hide-bound Soviet generals to recognize that large armoured formations were a necessity in modern warfare. The Red Army hastily began reforming its mechanized corps in June 1940 and a year later it had 29 in its order of battle, although they were still in the process of forming.

Most of the Soviet mechanized corps performed poorly in the opening stages of the German invasion of the Soviet Union in June 1941, and all were destroyed or disbanded by the time that the Soviet winter counter-offensive began in December 1941. Lacking large armoured units, the Red Army tried to re-introduce Deep Operations via stone soup methods, using improvised mobile groups based on brigades of light tanks, cavalry, ski troops and assorted paratrooper units, but these failed to achieve any successful deep penetrations. Realizing that decisive results were unlikely without the proper forces, the Red Army leadership accepted that the only kind of Deep Operations that were feasible for the moment were raiding operations to disrupt German rear areas.

Russian concepts of raiding operations were traditionally based on mounted cavalry operations, particularly Cossack units and the kind of fluid operations conducted on the steppes during the Russian Civil War. This experience was of limited value in World War II, since mounted units had very few logistical requirements compared with a mechanized corps. Unfortunately, many older Red Army officers remained wedded to the traditional cavalry doctrine of raiding, and made little effort to understand mechanized warfare. Widespread ignorance among senior Red Army commanders about the logistical requirements of mechanized units was a particular sore point. During the first year of the war on the Eastern Front, the Red Army conducted several corps-size cavalry raids behind German lines, including General-polkovnik (Colonel-General) Oka I. Gorodovikov's raid in July 1941, Major-General Lev M. Dovator's raid in August–September 1941 and Lieutenant-General Pavel Belov's raid in January–February 1942. Although these raids inflicted some disruption upon German lines of communication, the cavalry units lacked the firepower to attack German strongpoints, such as fortified towns or airbases. Typically, the cavalry corps was only able to impose temporary disruption upon German road/rail traffic and could not seize any key terrain or critical facilities. By early 1942, it was obvious to most of the Red Army leadership that the traditional cavalry corps was ill-suited to Deep Operations.

30 NOVEMBER 1942

Fiebig establishes headquarters at Tatsinskaya

Even before the winter counter-offensive had run its course, the Red Army laid plans to raise a new wave of tank corps in order to conduct proper Deep Operations in the summer of 1942. Between April and July 1942, a total of 25 tank corps were created, each with three tank brigades, one motorized infantry brigade and a battalion of Katyusha multiple rocket launchers. Yet unlike the German Panzer divisions, the Soviet tank corps were weak in terms of organic tube artillery and support elements. Two of the new tank corps received their combat debut in Marshal Semyon Timoshenko's offensive at Kharkov in May 1942, but the results were catastrophic: the 21st Tank Corps was destroyed and the 23rd Tank Corps was badly mauled. Attempting to conduct Deep Operations without air superiority and with inadequately trained and poorly equipped tanks corps proved to be a disaster. Yet the Red Army leadership recognized that it needed to conduct the kind of high-intensity mobile warfare that the Germans practised with their Panzer divisions, and they resolved to attempt Deep Operations again under more favourable conditions.

INITIAL STRATEGY

By late November 1942, the Soviet Stavka was aware that the German airlift was in progress, and that this action could delay the destruction of the Stalingrad pocket. So the Soviet Air Force (VVS) was directed to conduct air raids against the primary airfields, Tatsinskaya and Morozovskaya. Beginning on 3 December, the 221st Bomber Aviation Division (BAD), equipped with American-built A-20B/C light bombers, conducted daylight raids on both airfields and was able to cause some damage and disruption. Raids on 8–9 December succeeded in destroying ten aircraft on the ground, including four Ju-52 transport planes. In addition, fuel and ammunition dumps near the airfield were also hit by the Soviet bombers. The 221st BAD continued the raids for another two weeks, despite poor weather conditions, and succeeded in damaging three Ju-86 transports at Tatsinskaya on 21 December. In response, the Luftwaffe reinforced its flak units protecting both bases and increased fighter cover, which made life increasingly difficult for the Soviet bombers. However, Soviet fighters proved far more effective at intercepting the German transport planes approaching the Stalingrad pocket than Soviet bombers proved at disrupting the airlift at its source. At least 50 Ju-52 transports were shot down en route to Stalingrad during the first month of the airlift. Soviet bombers also proved incapable of seriously interdicting the main rail line that supported both the airlift and Heeresgruppe Don's new defensive line on the Chir River. On its own, Soviet airpower lacked the means to either stop the German airlift or disrupt the build-up for *Wintergewitter*.

One of the Stavka's most brilliant staff officers, Colonel-General Aleksandr M. Vasilevsky, was already supervising the reduction of the Stalingrad pocket and he was tasked to develop the follow-on plans to Operation *Uranus*, which would complete the German defeat in southern Russia. Between 24 November and 2 December, Vasilevsky outlined the basic plan for Operation *Saturn*, which would use the Southwest Front's 1st, 2nd and 3rd Guard Armies and the 5th Tank Army to destroy all Axis forces along the Middle Don and Chir River, as a precursor to overrunning the airlift airfields and then pushing on towards Rostov.

The Soviet Air Force (VVS) conducted a number of small-scale air raids on Tatsinskaya airfield with American-made A-20C bombers and inflicted some damage, but could not shut down the Stalingrad airlift. The limited ability of the 17th Air Army to conduct deep interdiction strikes also failed to interfere with von Manstein's efforts to transfer his Panzer reserves to deal with Badanov's tank raid. (Nik Cornish, AO 19)

Although mindful of the Red Army's limitations, Vasilevsky hoped to incorporate some elements of Deep Operations theory, including mobile raids into the German rear areas to sever their lines of communication. Once the basic concept was approved by the Stavka, Vasilevsky turned detailed planning for the offensive over to Colonel-General Nikolai N. Voronov, an artilleryman and Deputy People's Commissar for Defence. Both Vasilevsky and Voronov had studied under Isserson at the Frunze Military Academy in Moscow, and were convinced that a successful Deep Operation could achieve decisive results. Voronov intended to begin Operation *Saturn* on 10 December, but it was delayed twice. German resistance at Stalingrad proved more determined than expected – perhaps due to the morale-lifting effects of the airlift and the impending relief operation – which compelled the Stavka to strip resources from Vatutin's Southwest Front, including the 2nd Guards Army. Furthermore, a vital preliminary operation by the Soviet 5th Tank to gain a lodgement across the Chir River failed on 7–10 December due to the tenacious defence conducted by the German XXXXVIII Panzerkorps.

Once *Wintergewitter* began, it became obvious that the Soviets lacked the resources to simultaneously repel the German counter-offensive, crush AOK 6 in Stalingrad and mount a large-scale offensive along the Don River. Instead, the Stavka decided to downsize Operation *Saturn* to meet the changed circumstances, resulting in Operation *Little Saturn*. Voronov had only three days to plan the revised operation, which relied upon Vatutin's Southwest Front to punch a relatively narrow hole in the front held by the Italian 8th Army, then to exploit southward with two tank corps. Three other tank corps would be used in the infantry support role. Voronov expected that these two tank corps would overrun Tatsinskaya and Morozovskaya

3 DECEMBER 1942

Start of Soviet bombing operations against Tatsinskaya

airfields on the fourth day of the offensive and that they would also cut the rail line that supported XXXXVIII Panzerkorps. The Soviet planners aimed to destroy the bulk of Armee Abteilung Hollidt as well as the Italians, and intended that the Deep Operation by these two tank corps would bring both the Luftwaffe airlift and *Wintergewitter* to an abrupt halt. Since the bulk of the infantry and artillery of the 1st and 3rd Guard Armies could only advance slowly behind the exploitation force, Vasilevsky initially conceived of the operation against Tatsinskaya and Morozovskaya airfields as raids, rather than as permanent seizures. In line with Isserson's original theories about the role of the ERU, once the airfields were neutralized, both raiding forces would return to link up with the vanguard of Vatutin's infantry armies and refit for follow-on operations.

Voronov's plan specified that 1st Guards Army would concentrate two guards rifle divisions and three tank corps (17th, 18th, 25th) in the Osetrovka bridgehead across the Don River and attack the seam between the Italian 8th Army's II and XXXV Army Corps. Once a penetration corridor through the enemy front-line defences was created, the 24th Tank Corps would join the 25th Tank Corps to mount a deep raid against the two main Luftwaffe airfields. Voronov also directed that the 3rd Guards Army would commit a mobile group, the 1st Guards Mechanized Corps, to support the raid on Morozovskaya airfield. Terrain and weather conditions favoured the raids, since the hard, cold ground but relatively light snow cover would enable rapid mechanized movement across the flat steppes. It seemed that the Red Army finally had the opportunity to execute the kind of Deep Operations that had not yet been possible in this war. The Soviet plan was relatively simple in concept, but attempting to push a large mechanized force up to 240km (149 miles) behind the enemy front line was unprecedented in modern warfare.

Two Ju-52 transports taking off for the run to Stalingrad. Even under the best of weather conditions – as seen here – Fliegerkorps VIII had difficulty generating more than 40–50 supply flights to 6. Armee per day, well below the required amount. (Ian Barter)

However, the Soviet concept for the raids was severely compromised by a number of planning assumptions made before it was launched. Vatutin's staff made relatively little provision for air and logistical support to the two exploitation tank corps once they reached the enemy's operational depth, but somehow took it for granted that those elements would occur naturally. Similarly, the question of long-distance command and control between 1st Guards Army and the two tank corps was also based upon overly optimistic assumptions. Furthermore, Badanov's corps was initially subordinate to Lieutenant-General Vasily I. Kuznetsov's 1st Guards Army, but in the terminal phase of the raid its subordination would shift to Lieutenant-General Dmitri D. Lelyushenko's 3rd Guards Army – which left plenty of room for coordination mistakes in a fast-moving mechanized operation. In fact, the exploitation force would be virtually on its own once it was committed.

Soviet cavalry raids during the 1941/42 winter counter-offensive had succeeded in disrupting German rear-area lines of communication, but the lightly armed troops lacked the ability to capture fortified towns or airbases. Learning from this, the Soviet Stavka decided that it needed to resurrect tank corps in the spring of 1942 to mount proper Deep Operations. (Nik Cornish, K92)

THE PLAN

Major-General Badanov and Major-General Pavlov were both informed in early December that their two tank corps were selected to be the exploitation force for 1st Guards Army, and that their ultimate objectives were the Luftwaffe airfields at Tatsinskaya and Morozovskaya. Neither general had much of a staff in their newly formed corps headquarters, and they relied primarily upon Southwest Front and 1st Guards Army to complete much of the planning for the raids. Badanov's chief of staff, Polkovnik (Colonel) Aleksei S. Burdeinyi, coordinated with the staff of the Southwest Front in order to prepare the 24th Tank Corps for its first major operation. The issue of coordination between 24th Tank Corps and the 17th Air Army was of particular concern during the planning process, so an air liaison officer was attached to Badanov's small staff. This officer was responsible for obtaining the proper signals instructions and codes in order for Badanov to request air support, as well as obtaining coloured signal flares and marker panels for the

Troops of the 306. Infanterie-Division en route to the front in late December 1942. After more than a year of quiet occupation duty in Belgium, these soldiers were suddenly exposed to the brutality of the Russian winter and assigned the impossible mission of stopping or delaying two Soviet tank corps driving toward Heeresgruppe Don's main lines of communication. (Ian Barter)

PETR P. PAVLOV (1898–1962)

Pavlov joined the Red Army in 1918 and saw considerable action fighting first the Whites in the Civil War and then the Poles. After the war, Pavlov spent over a dozen years in the cavalry before switching to the new tank branch in 1932. During the next seven years, Pavlov was directly involved in training the first generation of Soviet tankers and raising the tank units. He was given command of a tank brigade in November 1940 and then the 41st Tank Division in the Kiev Military District in March 1941. When the German invasion began three months later, Pavlov's division was heavily engaged and was eventually surrounded and destroyed at Kiev. Pavlov successfully escaped the Kiev encirclement, however, and was transferred to the Volkhov Front, where he served in the 46th Tank Brigade during the Soviet counter-offensive at Tikhvin. He remained with the Volkhov Front until July 1942, in charge of armour in the 59th Army.

On 13 July 1942, Pavlov took command of the 25th Tank Corps and took part in the defensive battles around Voronezh, before being assigned a Deep Operation raiding mission for Operation *Little Saturn*. After his failure to capture Morozovskaya airfield, Pavlov's 25th Tank Corps was not withdrawn for rebuilding, but instead committed to a second Deep Operation during Operation *Gallop* in February 1943. This poorly planned operation fell victim to von Manstein's 'Backhand Blow' counter-offensive, which smashed four exposed Soviet tank corps, including Pavlov's. After his corps was destroyed, Pavlov was wounded and captured. He spent two years in German captivity before escaping in 1945 and joining the French partisans. Pavlov made his way back to the Soviet Union in April 1945, but was briefly imprisoned before finally returning to duty. Although he received General Staff training after the war, Pavlov never held another important assignment and retired in 1950.

tanks. Although the preparations were conducted in haste, the issue of ground–air coordination appeared resolved.

Burdeinyi also worked with the 1st Guards Army staff to organize two map exercises prior to the raid, to test interaction between rifle units, the tank corps, artillery and aviation. These exercises, however, involved only higher-level commanders – in order to preserve operational security – and apparently were not realistic enough to detect any serious coordination problems. In addition, Burdeinyi arranged for Badanov and his brigade commanders to cross the Don into the Osetrovka bridgehead in order to conduct a leader's reconnaissance of their expected breakthrough corridor.

16 DECEMBER 1942

306. Infanterie-Division occupies positions between Rostov and Morozovskaya

Intelligence support for the operation appeared to be adequate. Information on the layout of the airfields was plentiful, since they had been in Soviet hands only five months previously and the VVS made regular overflights of both. None of the men involved in planning the raid – Vasilevsky, Voronov or Vatutin – expected significant German ground opposition around the airfields, since they knew that Heeresgruppe Don could barely hold its tenuous front line even before Operation *Little Saturn* began. Once the Italian 8th Army was defeated, they expected the 24th and 25th Tank Corps to have a relatively unopposed advance all the way to both airfields. Vasilevsky and Voronov believed that a full tank corps should be able to handle whatever Luftwaffe flak units and other sundry rear-echelon units were located at each airfield, and then be able to fight their way back to Soviet lines. Burdeinyi coordinated with the Southwest Front staff, who promised to provide daily intelligence updates via radio to 24th Tank Corps as it marched upon its objective.

Unknown to the men planning the raids on Tatsinskaya and Morozovskaya airfields, the Germans were beginning to react to the crisis caused by the Stalingrad debacle and were rushing reinforcements to the east. In Ghent, Belgium, the German 306. Infanterie-Division had spent a year of quiet occupation duty in the West when it was suddenly alerted that it was being transferred to Heeresgruppe Don. Von Manstein intended to initially concentrate this full-strength division around Morozovskaya airfield before committing it to strengthen his thin line along the Chir River. Since the current aged commander of the 306. Infanterie-Division was retiring and the divisional staff lacked recent combat experience, Manstein wanted a proven commander and staff put in charge of this important unit.

On 11 December, Generalleutnant Georg Pfeiffer, commander of the 94. Infanterie-Division, was flown out of the Stalingrad pocket with his divisional staff. Pfeiffer immediately set up a divisional command post at Ssibirki, 7km (4 miles) southwest of Morozovskaya, and prepared to receive the first echelons of the 306. Infanterie-Division. The 306. Infanterie-Division arrived piecemeal in six echelons, and by 16 December was spread out along the rail line between Rostov and Morozovskaya. Pfeiffer began forming the sub-units into mixed *Kampfgruppen* (battlegroups) as they arrived, and he anticipated that the entire division would be assembled by Christmas. Focused primarily on Stalingrad and the Italian front along the Don, Soviet intelligence failed to detect these developments in the German rear area.

On the northern side of the Don near Nizhniy Mamon, Badanov concentrated the 24th Tank Corps in an assembly area and completed final preparations for their role in *Little Saturn*. Although each tank corps had a nominal strength of about 7,500 troops and 158 tanks, this was actually not much larger than the Canadian raiding force (6,000 troops and 58 tanks) used in the Dieppe raid four months earlier. However, while the Canadian force did not have to worry much about logistics during their one-day operation, the logistics of mounting a Deep Operation that would take at least four days to reach objectives that were 230km (144 miles) behind enemy lines were daunting. Badanov's and Pavlov's tank corps were

Generalleutnant Martin Fiebig (1891–1947), the commander of VIII Fliegerkorps and the man responsible for running the airlift from Tatsinskaya airfield. Fiebig had left the military after World War I and worked for Lufthansa, until joining the newly formed Luftwaffe in 1934. He led the He-111 bomber group Kampfgeschwader 4 (KG 4) in the Polish and French campaigns, but was shot down and captured by the Dutch on the first day of Case Yellow (the invasion of France and Low Countries) in 1940. Fiebig was an aviation leader with a talent for organization, but he was out of his depth in the crisis atmosphere during the Stalingrad debacle and failed to prepare Tatsinskaya airbase either for evacuation or defence. (Bundesarchiv, Bild 1011-529-2383-37, Fotograf: Krempl)

A Soviet T-34 tank crew receives a briefing on an upcoming mission under idealized conditions. The Red Army preferred to use its armour in tightly scripted operations due to its tankers' low standards of training and experience compared with their German counterparts, but Badanov did not have this luxury during the Tatsinskaya raid. Instead, his tankers embarked on the raid with only a rough idea about the terrain and the enemy forces at the objective, and were forced to improvise as the 24th Tank Corps did not reach Tatsinskaya as a cohesive force. (Author)

each given two loads of fuel and two basic loads of ammunition, as well as five days' rations. These extra supplies amounted to over 100 tons each of fuel and ammunition, but the hauling capability of each tank corps was quite limited, with most truck space being used to carry the four battalions of infantrymen. Fuel consumption was clearly going to be a problem for the raiding forces, since they would burn through more than one load of fuel just to reach their objectives, leaving little left for manoeuvre or the return to Soviet lines. Driving across the steppes, rather than on roads, would avoid most German blocking units but would further increase the fuel consumption as well as the wear and tear on the vehicles, particularly the vital supply trucks.

The Red Army still had very limited experience with conducting Deep Operations in wartime and pre-war exercises had been held under ideal conditions in the summer months. Badanov's raid, therefore, suffered from two main planning flaws. Firstly, the Southwest Front staff did not properly evaluate the effects of weather and terrain upon Badanov's ability to manoeuvre – they simply assumed that he could adhere to pre-war calculations and move his tank corps at a rate of more than 50km (31 miles) per day. Secondly, the planners chose to use aspects of Isserson's pre-war doctrine on Deep Operations with an ERU, but they ignored his warnings that a mechanized raiding force was good for only about three days before its strength eroded and it became vulnerable to encirclement by enemy reserves. While Isserson recognized the fragility of a tank corps operating deep behind enemy lines, the Southwest Front staff confidently assumed that these admonitions did not apply in December 1942 due to the weakness of Heeresgruppe Don.

THE RAID

The Approach March, 16–23 December 1942

On the morning of 16 December 1942, Vatutin's Southwest Front began Operation *Little Saturn* with a 90-minute artillery barrage against the Italian 8th Army positions facing the Osetrovka bridgehead. Then Soviet rifle divisions attacked the seam between the Italian II and XXXV Army Corps. However, the Italians – aided by a timely counter-attack by the German 27. Panzer-Division – held for nearly two days until finally breaking under the Soviet onslaught. Badanov's corps spent the first day of *Little Saturn* north of the Don in its assembly area, but on the second day Vatutin directed it to begin crossing into the bridgehead. Although the Don was frozen, engineer units from 1st Guards Army had built bridges across the river, which were used by Badanov's corps to cross into the Osetrovka bridgehead. In order to avoid congestion at the bridges, Badanov divided his corps into two echelons, with the 54th and 130th Tank Brigades in the first echelon and 4th Guards Tank and 24th Motorized Rifle brigades in the second. The first echelon of Badanov's corps began crossing the Don at 1130hrs on 17 December, followed by the second echelon at 1430hrs. By 1830hrs, the entire corps was across the Don and ready to be committed to action.

Due to the unexpected Italian/German resistance, Vatutin was forced to commit three of his tank corps, including Pavlov's 25th, to support the infantry breakthrough attacks. Finally, by the evening of 17 December, Vatutin recognized that the time had arrived to begin the exploitation phase of the operation. Badanov and Pavlov were alerted to begin their Deep Operations on the next morning. At 0200hrs on 18 December, Badanov's corps conducted a forward passage of lines through the 4th Guards Rifle Corps and advanced southward into the snow-filled void.

With a 15km (9-mile) wide breach torn between the two Italian corps, the way was clear for a clean advance into the enemy's rear areas. Due to its commitment to help with the breakthrough, Pavlov's corps advanced well ahead of Badanov's, but ran into numerous fragments of enemy resistance.

16 DECEMBER 1942

Operation *Little Saturn* commences with artillery barrage

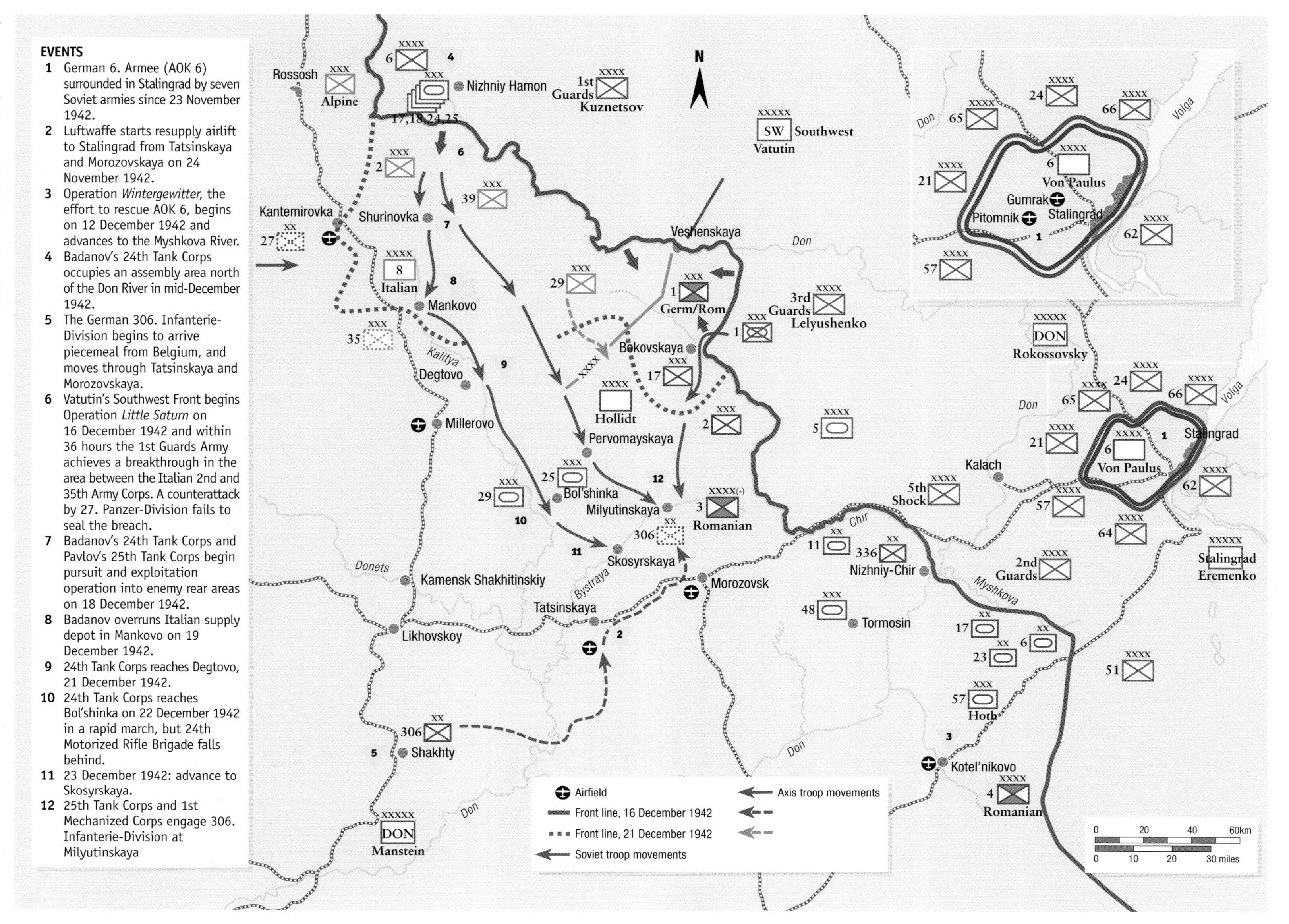

The Approach March, 16–23 December 1942

Oddly, Vatutin had designated this phase of 24th Tank Corps' operation as a pursuit, so rather than avoid unnecessary enemy contact en route to his raid objective, Badanov was ordered to defeat these enemy pockets of resistance. Once clear of the breakthrough zone, he continued to march his corps in the same two echelons, in column of brigades, with a reinforced vanguard from the 130th Tank Brigade and a mortar battery from the 24th Motorized Rifle Brigade. On each flank of the corps, he deployed reconnaissance teams consisting of one to three T-34 tanks, one or two T-70 light tanks and some embarked infantry. The vulnerable support units were tucked inside the middle of the formation.

The column was immense – initially about 5km (3 miles) long and 1.5–2km (0.9–1.2 miles) wide – but there were few Germans or Italians in the area to see it. Despite light enemy resistance in front of them, the 24th Tank Corps first had to cross the frozen Boguchar River and then, later on the first day, cross the Bogucharka River near the town of Shurinovka. Between 0200hrs and 2000hrs, the corps advanced 25km (15 miles) and fought several minor actions against enemy rearguards. Fighters from the 17th Air Army provided air cover over the advancing 24th Tank Corps on the first day, but as Badanov's troops moved further away from Soviet air bases, the cover gradually faded away.

Although his overall mission was to conduct a raid, Badanov's instructions from Southwest Front also assigned him a number of intermediate objectives,

The 24th Tank Corps marched for four days across the frozen steppe. As vehicles broke down, some tanks picked up riders. The days were gloomy, cold, short and monotonous. The crews were frozen most of the time and maintenance was extremely difficult. (Author)

designed to assist the advance of 1st Guards Army. After laagering for the night of 18 December near Shurinovka, Badanov set off early the next morning and advanced southward along the east side of the Kalitya River. The Southwest Front had ordered him to seize a large Italian supply dump near the towns of Man'kovo and Chertkovo, so he dispatched Colonel Stepan Nesterov's 130th Tank Brigade to approach Man'kovo at high speed from the north, while Colonel Vasily Polyarkov's 54th Tank Brigade bypassed the town and set up blocking positions south of it along the main road. As the 54th Tank Brigade manoeuvred in a valley near Man'kovo, it was spotted by a formation of German He-111 bombers. Due to the 1m (3ft) deep snow, even the T-34s could only advance slowly, and they were exposed to a bombing attack that damaged and destroyed a number of vehicles. Nevertheless, Polyarkov succeeded in encircling the town, while Nesterov advanced directly into it. Despite having two batteries of anti-aircraft guns in Man'kovo, the Italians put up negligible resistance, and Nesterov was able to kill or capture 800 Italian soldiers as well as liberating several hundred Soviet prisoners of war. The Soviet tankers also netted a large part of the Italian 8th Army's quartermaster stocks in Man'kovo, including food, fuel and 300 wheeled vehicles. Badanov took some of the more serviceable trucks to replenish his own vehicle losses, while leaving the Italian prisoners under guard of the released Soviet POWs, to await 1st Guards Army.

Meanwhile, Kapitan (Captain) Mikhail E. Nechayev was ordered to conduct a raid on the Chertkovo train station west of Man'kovo with his

The T-70 light tank was less suited to a long-distance tank raid than the robustly designed T-34 medium tank. The T-70 was a wartime expedient, powered by two truck engines and with only a two-man crew. (Author)

THE 24TH TANK CORPS

The 24th Tank Corps was formed by the Southern Front in April 1942, but remained in reserve during the disastrous Kharkov Offensive in May. The corps was formed from existing brigades and by June 1942 it comprised the 4th Guards, 54th and 130th Tank Brigades and the 24th Motorized Rifle Brigade. The 4th Guards Tank Brigade (originally the 132nd Tank Brigade) was the most experienced subordinate unit and had served well in the 1941/42 Soviet winter counter-offensive. The 130th Tank Brigade was badly mauled at the battle of Kharkov and was rebuilt during the summer months. Each tank brigade was assigned 32 T-34 and 21 T-70 tanks, although the number of operational tanks at the start of the raid was 90 per cent. Prior to Operation *Little Saturn*, the tank brigades in the 24th Tank Corps had served primarily in the infantry-support role and had no experience or training with raiding or Deep Operations. Instead, they had to learn high-intensity mechanized warfare on the march.

The 24th Motorized Rifle Brigade was designed to enable the corps to hold objectives that the tanks had captured. In addition to three truck-mounted rifle battalions, it had an artillery battalion with 12 ZIS-3 76mm field guns, a mortar battalion with 12 82mm and 6 120mm mortars, 12 37mm anti-aircraft guns, 12 45mm anti-tank guns, a company of submachine-gunners and a reconnaissance company. Prior to Operation *Little Saturn*, the brigade received infantry replacements from both airborne (VDV) and naval infantry detachments to add stiffening to its rifle battalions.

The corps had a number of sub-units attached from Southwest Front, including the 413th Guards Mortar Battalion with eight BM-13 multiple rocket launchers, an anti-aircraft regiment, an engineer company and an NKVD detachment. The support units included the 30th Separate Truck Company assigned to haul fuel, the 156th Mobile Tank Repair Base and the 112th Mobile Auto Repair Base. For command and control, the corps relied on a single long-range RSB-F HF radio transmitter mounted on a GAZ-AAA truck, which enabled it to transmit with higher headquarters up to a maximum range of 160km (100 miles). Each tank brigade was equipped with a few command vehicles with HF radios, but none had ranges greater than 25–30km (15½–19 miles). Thus during mobile Deep Operations, Soviet command control in tank corps became problematic as units moved beyond effective radio range.

Prior to the raid, the 24th Tank Corps received two units of ammunition (about 111 tons), two units of fuel (about 109 tons) and five days of rations. Altogether, this amounted to more than 230 tons of supplies, but the brigade had only 50 per cent of its authorized trucks which meant that its logistical hauling capacity was at best 75 tons. Given this shortfall, every tank and vehicle had to be overloaded with fuel drums, boxes of ammunition and food.

Overall, the corps and its various attachments had an authorized strength of 7,060 troops, but since most sub-units were at 70 per cent manning, the total number actually involved in the raid was about 5,000. At the start of the raid, the corps fielded approximately 144 tanks and 300 trucks, plus some armoured cars.

Key commanders in the 24th Tank Corps were:

- Chief of Staff: Colonel Aleksei S. Burdeinyi
- Commissar: Colonel Ivan Z. Bakhtin
- Chief of Operations: Colonel Sergey Lavrentiev
- 4th Guards Tank Brigade: Colonel Georgy I. Kolypov
- 54th Tank Brigade: Colonel Vasily M. Polyakov
- 130th Tank Brigade: Colonel Stepan K. Nesterov
- 24th Motorized Rifle Brigade: Colonel Vasily S. Savchenko

Tank Strength in the 24th Tank Corps, December 1942

Tanks	Authorized	18 December	23 December	24 December	28 December
T-34	96	*c.* 87	*c.* 60	39	*c.* 8
T-70	63	*c.* 57	*c.* 40	19	*c.* 3
Total	159	*c.* 144	> 100	58	11

2nd Battalion of the 130th Tank Brigade, and destroy the train station and rail bridge. Another action occurred near the town of Kuteynikovo, where the 4th Guards Tank Brigade inflicted more than 400 casualties on other enemy rear-echelon units, but suffered 46 killed itself. Badanov succeeded in eliminating most of the enemy support units in his path, but he had advanced less than 25km (15½ miles) on 19 December and was forced to

Soviet tankers on the Southwest Front kneel in front of their factory-fresh T-34 tanks during an induction ceremony for the newly formed tank corps in April 1942. While numerous tank brigades remained for the infantry-support role, the tank corps were specifically created to conduct Deep Operations. (RIA Novosti, 60427)

consolidate for the night at Man'kovo. Once the corps support elements closed up to the town, Badanov ordered his tank units to refuel and replenish their ammunition.

Moving nearly 500 vehicles in a compact mass across the snow-laden steppes proved difficult even without enemy resistance. As air support from 17th Air Army dwindled after leaving Man'kovo, Badanov had to disperse his corps into smaller groups to reduce their vulnerability to air attack, but this made command and control more difficult as the formation spread out.

Movement was particularly difficult due to the short winter days and the limited road network. At this time of year, sunrise was around 0700hrs and sunset about 1530hrs, giving only 8½ hours of daylight for movement each day. Soviet trucks such as the GAZ-AAA had difficulty keeping up with the T-34 tanks, and the heavy loads of fuel and ammunition they were carrying stressed their suspension systems.

Driving for hours across the frozen and monotonous steppe caused many drivers to fall asleep, resulting in vehicles bogging down in snowdrifts or ditches. With snow blowing and limited light, visibility was poor and navigation over the featureless terrain proved difficult. Crew fatigue increased rapidly after the first few days, and since the Red Army had trained only specific personnel as drivers, rotating drivers proved problematic. While the T-34 tank had an internal heater that afforded some warmth to its crews, most of the personnel in trucks had no such facility and were carried along as a cargo of half-frozen flesh. Badanov mandated short rest stops every hour or so, which helped to keep his crews going.

17 DECEMBER 1942

1130–1830hrs Badanov's corps crosses the Don

By the end of the second day, more and more vehicles were beginning to suffer mechanical defects and had to be abandoned. Normal tank maintenance was difficult in the snow, causing oil leaks and broken track pins to go unnoticed until problems became obvious. Crews were reluctant to fall behind, fearing being left alone on the steppe behind enemy lines, so they nursed their vehicles along. Even during nightly rest stops, engines had to be kept idling to charge batteries and to avoid cold-start problems in the morning, but this measure further increased fuel consumption. Throughout the approach march, Badanov had to monitor his fuel consumption rate carefully in order to ensure that he had enough fuel to reach the objective and return to Soviet lines. Thus rather than the bold 50–100km (31–62 miles) per day advance envisioned by Isserson, Badanov was forced to crawl along at about 25km (15½ miles) per day in order to conserve fuel and keep his formation together. Travelling at night behind enemy lines was not really an option, since more vehicles would be lost through driver fatigue and the formation could break up into fragmented units. Meanwhile, Pavlov's corps had advanced well ahead of Badanov's corps – nearly a day's march ahead – but was running into small firefights with retreating fragments of the Italian 8th Army.

At the headquarters of Heeresgruppe Don, von Manstein was aware that Vatutin had achieved a major breakthrough in the Italian sector, but he had to deal with multiple crises as the front along the Don collapsed. In order to protect the airbases supporting the Stalingrad airlift and the vital rail line to Tormosin, Manstein ordered what was left of the Romanian 3rd Army to establish blocking positions north of Morozovskaya to stop any Soviet raiding forces. The main defence was based on Gruppe Spang from the 8. Luftwaffen-Feld-Division (8th Luftwaffe Field Division), which created a

Badanov's corps included the 413th Guards Mortar Battalion with eight BM-13 Katyusha multiple rocket launchers. Although this battalion provided the corps with a high volume of firepower, it was essentially a one-shot advantage and did not compare with the tube artillery available to a Panzer division. (RIA Novosti, 303882)

thin screen between Milyutinskaya and the Chir River. Pfeiffer was ordered to feed in the 306. Infanterie-Division to reinforce Group Spang at Milyutinskaya as it arrived. This sector was regarded as the most likely enemy avenue of approach and thus the most critical. However, to cover the wide-open Bystraya River front north of Tatsinskaya, Pfeiffer formed four small ad hoc *Kampfgruppen* from odds and ends in the rear, including soldiers returning from leave in Germany. Kampfgruppe Tzschöckell, under Oberst Paul Tzschöckell, the 70-year old commander of Nebelwerfer-Regiment 53, guarded the extreme left flank of Gruppe Pfeiffer around Kryukov. In the centre near the town of Skosyrskaya, on the south side of the Bystraya River, Pfeiffer placed two small *Kampfgruppen*. The first was Kampfgruppe von Burgsdorf under Oberstleutnant Kurt von Burgsdorf, commander of Panzerjäger Abteilung 16 (16th Tank-Destroyer Battalion), and was a mixed group of soldiers from the 16. Panzer-Division. The other unit was Kampfgruppe von Heinemann under Major Lothar von Heinemann, the Ia (Operations Officer) from VIII Fliegerkorps, and formed from Luftwaffe signal troops from Luftnachrichten-Regiment 38 (38th Air Intelligence Regiment) and some flak crews taken from Tatsinskaya. Heinemann's makeshift unit was the strongest of the blocking detachments, with 200 men, six 8.8cm flak guns and 12 2cm flak guns. Pfeiffer did not expect much enemy activity in this sector and saw these units merely as a screening force, while he committed the bulk of the 306. Infanterie-Division north of Morozovskaya.

As the Germans reacted frantically to the Soviet breakthrough, Badanov and Pavlov steadily continued to advance upon their objectives. Although the original plan had specified that the raids on Tatsinskaya and Morozovskaya airfields would occur on the fourth day of the offensive, the practical difficulties of marching a large mechanized formation over 200km (124 miles) across the steppe in winter demolished this timetable. After three days of marching, Badanov's first echelon brigades reached Degtovo and scattered some rearguards from the Romanian 11th Infantry Division. However, the second echelon and the support units were lagging further back each day, and the corps formation had stretched out to more than 16km (10 miles) in length. A few retreating columns of the Italian 9th Motorized Division *Pasubio* were encountered and prisoners taken, which forced Badanov to detach some of his infantry to remain with them until relieved by 1st Guards Army.

Far more serious were the increasing problems with radio communications with Front headquarters due to the increasing distance. The 24th Tank Corps had a single long-range RSB-F HF radio transmitter mounted on a GAZ-AAA truck, which enabled it to transmit with higher headquarters up to a maximum range of 160km (99 miles). Yet maximum range was achieved only by stopping and erecting a long whip antenna. When transmitting on the march, the RSB-F only had a maximum range of 30km (19 miles). Badanov ordered the radio truck to set up the long antenna during the nightly halts to transmit daily situation updates but otherwise he was out of communication with Vatutin for most of each day. When he contacted Southwest Front headquarters on the

22 DECEMBER 1942

4th Guards Tank Brigade seizes Ilyinka

evening of 20 December, he received a directive from Vatutin that he was to reach Tatsinskaya no later than 23 December. Still in the lead, Pavlov was ordered to conduct the raid on Morozovskaya on 22 December, in conjunction with the 1st Mechanized Corps. Due to this directive, Badanov quickened the pace of march and reached the town of Bol'shinka by 2000hrs on 21 December. The faster pace, however, caused the 24th Tank Corps echelons to become further separated and also increased the rate of vehicles lost to breakdowns. In spite of his troops' effort, Badanov realized that he still had another 56km (35 miles) more to go to reach the objective.

On the morning of 22 December, Badanov sent Colonel Georgy I. Kolypov's 4th Guards Tank Brigade ahead to seize the town of Ilyinka, then followed with the rest of the corps. Badanov spent some time re-organizing the corps at Ilyinka and prepared for the final phase of the approach march. Soviet air support had ended after Degtovo, and communications with Southwest Front were usually only possible during nightly halts. Resuming the advance before dawn on the morning of 23 December, the 24th Tank Corps continued marching towards the south-east. One last obstacle, the

The 306. Infanterie-Division was forced to occupy hasty fighting positions virtually off the line of march in order to react to the sudden Soviet advance brought about by Operation *Little Saturn*. Here, German infantrymen form a blocking position north of Morozovskaya airfield. (Ian Barter)

Bystraya River, lay ahead. Badanov sent the 54th and 130th Tank Brigades and a motorized rifle company on a direct route to cross the river at Skosyrskaya, but sent the 4th Guards Tank Brigade to reconnoitre an alternative crossing site near Kryukov. Colonel Vasily Savchenko's 24th Motorized Rifle Brigade lagged considerably behind the main column, nursing the slow-moving support units.

23 DECEMBER 1942

0600hrs Milyutinskaya taken by Soviet forces

Meanwhile, Pavlov's 25th Tank Corps advanced steadily towards the Bystraya River, with the 1st Guards Mechanized Corps not far behind. Pavlov had also been instructed to defeat enemy rearguards en route to his objective, and he succeeded in overrunning the retreating Romanian 11th Infantry Division near Pervomayskoye on 22–23 December. After this victory, he intended to sprint the last 30–40km (19–25 miles) to Morozovskaya, but first he had to cross the Bystraya at Milyutinskaya. However, his lead tank brigade unexpectedly bumped into part of the 306. Infanterie-Division, which Pfeiffer had dispatched just in time to form a blocking position on the hills above the town. The German *Kampfgruppe* had a platoon of 7.5cm PaK guns and managed to knock out nine Soviet tanks at the cost of one of their own guns. Instead of bypassing this resistance nest and looking for another crossing site, Pavlov decided to deploy his corps on line and go after the German blocking unit.

After a year of quiet occupation duty in Belgium, the *Landsers* of the 306. Infanterie-Division were suddenly exposed to the violence of a Soviet tank corps on the attack. A battalion of the Grenadier-Regiment 580 were overrun by Pavlov's tankers, and the Germans later admitted heavy losses. Rather than skirt around Gruppe Spang's virtually undefended western flank, Pavlov decided to crush what appeared to be a weak defence, but in the process he lost sight of his true objective. Most of a day was wasted in this indecisive battle with Gruppe Spang, an engagement that consumed the 25th Tank Corps' limited fuel and ammunition reserves. Gruppe Spang appealed to Fliegerkorps VIII for air support, and due to the lack of Soviet fighter cover a dozen Ju-87 Stuka dive-bombers from I Gruppe, Sturzkampfgeschwader 2 (I/St.G. 2) began to chip away at Pavlov's exposed corps. Eventually, the balance tipped in favour of the Soviet side when elements of the 1st Guards Mechanized Corps arrived to reinforce Pavlov's attack. Milyutinskaya was seized by 0600hrs on 23 December and Pavlov moved his corps across the Bystraya River, but his forces were now quite depleted.

Unaware of Pavlov's deteriorating situation, Badanov's corps approached the Bystraya near the town of Skosyrskaya on the afternoon of 23 December. Given the short winter days, it was already dark by the time that the column approached the Bystraya, which prevented a proper reconnaissance by the advance guard. A bridge crossed the 50m (164ft) wide river at this point, and even though the waters were frozen the riverbed served as a handy anti-tank ditch. Von Heinemann's Luftwaffe signal troops had also managed to lay some Tellermine 35 anti-tank mines in the riverbed.

Luftwaffe reconnaissance aircraft spotted Badanov's tank column as it neared the town and probably alerted Burgsdorf and von Heinemann. Although von Heinemann's troops were not particularly suited to the ground defence role, they had selected favourable firing positions for their 8.8cm and 2cm flak guns overlooking the bridge and other likely crossing sites. Hearing the sound of Nesterov's advance guard platoons approaching the bridge in the dwindling light, the Luftwaffe flak gunners engaged and destroyed some of the lead tanks. Soviet tankers mistook the 8.8cm gun flashes for tank fire and they reported to Nesterov that there were German tanks in Skosyrskaya. The T-34s looked for cover and then began a protracted gun duel with the 8.8cm flak guns, using up much of their main gun ammunition in the process.

Eventually, Nesterov realized that his brigade could not remain in the German 'kill zone' for too long without becoming combat ineffective, so he decided to mount a hasty attack across the bridge without benefit of artillery support and with only limited infantry on hand. With the T-34s in the lead, the 130th Tank Brigade surged across the bridge and into the northern edge of the town. Although many of Nesterov's tanks and vehicles were damaged, the Luftwaffe troops were not up to close-quarter fighting with a full Soviet tank brigade, and they began to waver. Eventually, the 130th Tank Brigade forced its way into the town, but due to the lack of infantry support, the battle dragged on for five hours. Both German *Kampfgruppen* finally decided to withdraw to the east and southeast around 2200hrs, but remained in the vicinity of the town. Badanov later claimed to have inflicted more than 1,000 casualties on the enemy at Skosyrskaya, but von Heinemann actually lost only 40 men in the retreat, plus five 8.8cm guns and ten 2cm guns abandoned. When Badanov arrived in the town, he was surprised how many vehicles had been damaged in the protracted action and how little fuel and ammunition his armoured spearhead still possessed.

Badanov was now only 27km (17 miles) from Tatsinskaya and he knew that it was decision time. The 24th Tank Corps was now badly spread out, with only the tank units on the south side of the Bystraya, but most of the 24th Motorized Rifle Brigade and the support units were still advancing towards the river. The fighting in Skosyrskaya had cost Badanov tanks, fuel and time. He preferred to refuel all three tank brigades by taking fuel from damaged vehicles and then push on to the objective, but that would mean a daylight march under air attack and against an alerted enemy. Under such conditions, he could expect a warm welcome at Tatsinskaya and probably all enemy aircraft evacuated before he arrived. Refuelling would take hours and cost him any remaining surprise. On the other hand, his scouts informed him that the two German *Kampfgruppen* were lingering nearby, and if Badanov left his support troops unprotected in Skosyrskaya, the enemy might return in the morning and destroy his remaining supplies. Faced with this critical dilemma, Badanov made the bold decision to push on to the objective as soon as possible with his tank brigades and the available combat support units, but to leave Colonel Savchenko's 24th Motorized Rifle Brigade and a tank company of 4th Guards Tank Brigade to finish clearing out the town and to shepherd the slow-moving truck columns to Tatsinskaya. Badanov made this decision on his own, since contact with Vatutin's headquarters was now irregular.

EVENTS

1. Gruppe Pfeiffer deploys four *ad hoc* Kampfgruppen to hold a screen line along the Bystraya River.
2. 24th Tank Corps approaches the Bystraya River in column of march. Badanov sends 4th Guards Tank Brigade to reconnoiter alternative crossing site near Kryukov.
3. 1700–2200hrs, 23 December 1942: 130th Tank Brigade fights its way into Skosyrskaya against Kampfgruppe von Heinemann. The German screening force withdraws after a five-hour fight.
4. After securing Skosyrskaya, Badanov decides not to wait for resupply or the 24th Motorized Rifle Brigade but instead pushes south toward the objective with his three tank brigades. The 4th Guards Tank Brigade is in reserve.
5. The 54th Tank Brigade is dispatched to envelop Tatsinskaya from the west.
6. The 130th Tank Brigade swings wide to strike the east side of the town and the airfield.
7. The 25th Tank Corps shoves its way past the 306. Infanterie-Division and its spearheads reach the village of Uryupin by 24 December, but are brought to a halt by Luftwaffe bombing.

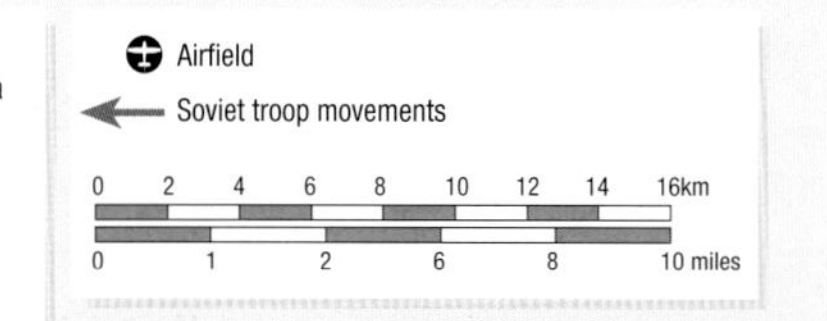

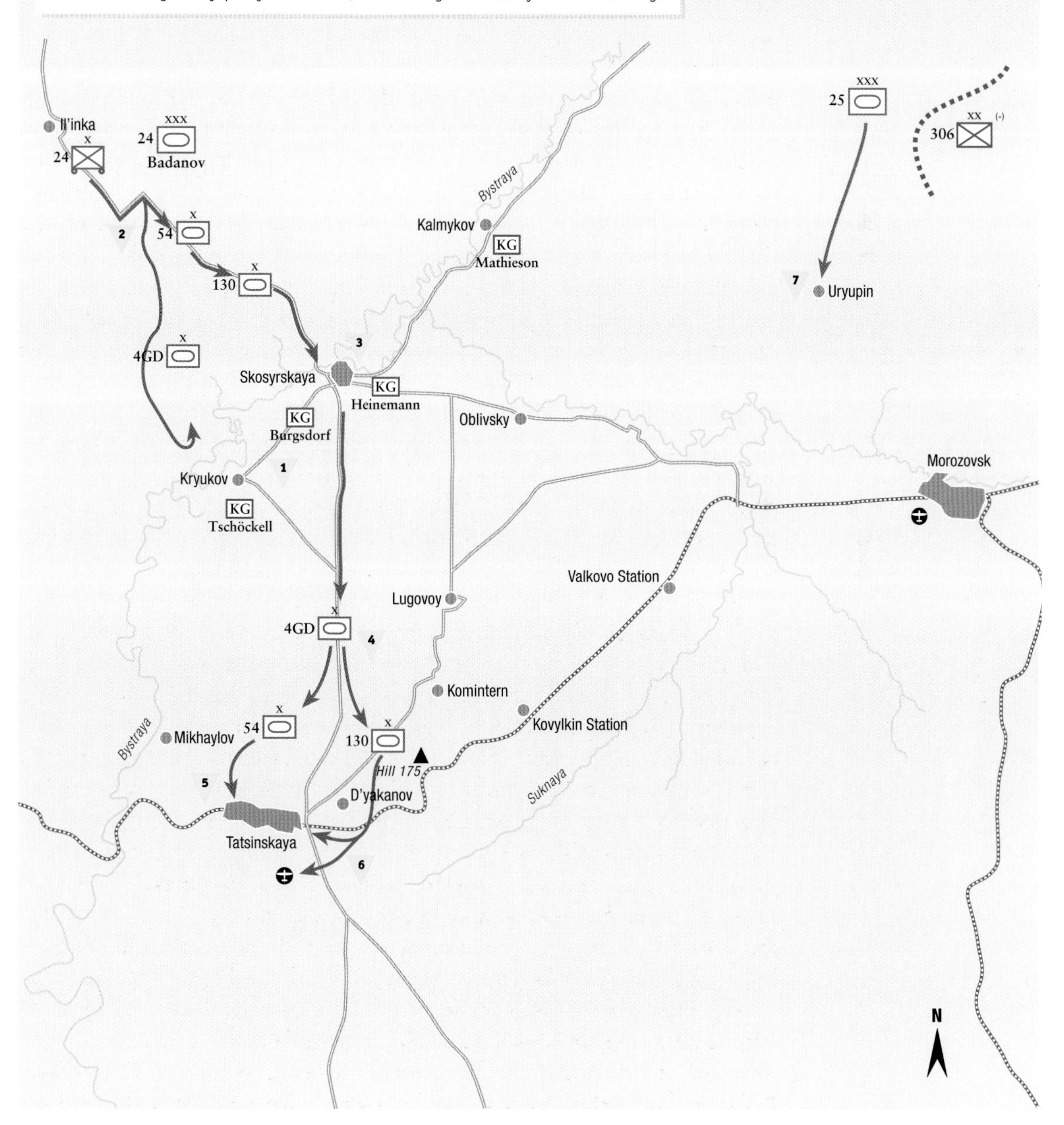

Movement to the Objective

After deciding to give the troops a couple of hours to rest in Skosyrskaya, Badanov met with his subordinates to assign specific tasks for each unit. Nesterov's 130th Tank Brigade, the main effort, would bypass the town of Tatsinskaya and occupy an attack position 4km (2½ miles) east of the airfield by 0600hrs. Kolypov's 4th Guards Tank Brigade, the supporting force, would occupy an attack position the same distance west of the airfield. A single rifle company of the 1st Battalion, 24th Motorized Rifle Brigade, as well as the 413th Guards Mortar Battalion and the 658th Anti-aircraft Regiment, would occupy positions 3km (2 miles) north of the town. The 54th Tank Brigade would remain in reserve north of the town, as well. Badanov would initiate the attack at 0730hrs by sending the coded radio signal '555'.

After this brief coordination, the tankers of the 24th Tank Corps mounted up just after midnight on 23/24 December and set out on the final leg of the raid. As Isserson toiled in a labour camp in Kazakhstan, Badanov's tankers were about to demonstrate the effectiveness of his theories to the Luftwaffe personnel at Tatsinskaya.

To hold the Bystraya River line, Gruppe Pfeiffer formed several ad hoc *Kampfgruppen* from Luftwaffe signal troops, Army smoke units and troops returning from leave in Germany, just before the Soviet 24th and 25th Tank Corps arrived. These troops had virtually no heavy weapons and provided little more than early warning to the airfields of Tatsinskaya and Morozovskaya. (Ian Barter)

The Attack, 24 December

At Tatsinskaya, Generalleutnant Martin Fiebig had been nervously watching the intermittent reports from Gruppe Spang and Gruppe Pfeiffer, and realized that Soviet armour could threaten his airfield with little advance warning. He kept pestering von Richtofen with requests to begin an orderly evacuation of the airfield, but Göring would not allow anything to disrupt the airlift to Stalingrad. Operation *Wintergewitter* had just ended, with Hoth's Panzers 46km (28½ miles) short of Stalingrad and German morale plummeting – this was not the time to pull the plug on the airlift. Hitler was hoping to restart the rescue operation once more reinforcements arrived from Heeresgruppe A in the Caucasus, so the airlift was a vital part of sustaining AOK 6 morale.

Officially, von Richtofen's hands were tied, but he sent his chief of staff, Oberst Herhudt von Rohden, to evaluate the situation at Tatsinskaya. Von Rohden instructed Fiebig to organize a ground defence force at Tatsinskaya from his flak crews and ground personnel, and authorized him to evacuate 30 Ju-52 transports and some of the ground personnel to Ssalsk; only about half the transports at Tatsinskaya were used for the Stalingrad airlift on any given day, and reducing the congestion on the airfield would facilitate an evacuation, if it came to that. However, Fiebig only dispatched nine Ju-52s to Ssalsk late on 23 December and four were destroyed in crash landings due to adverse weather. On account of these losses, Fiebig hesitated to evacuate any more aircraft.

In order to buck up morale, Hitler awarded Fiebig the Oak Leaves to his *Ritterkreuz des Eisernen Kreuzes* (Knight's Cross of the Iron Cross). Despite just being awarded one of the Third Reich's highest awards for bravery, Fiebig went into near panic on the night of 23 December when he found out from von Heinemann that Soviet tanks were at Skosyrskaya. He appealed once more to von Richtofen for permission to evacuate, but was again refused. Safe in Berlin, Göring ordered that his Luftwaffe men would 'stand fast' at Tatsinskaya and that evacuation was not authorized unless Soviet tanks were firing on the runway.

At Heeresgruppe Don headquarters, von Manstein was sufficiently concerned about the threat to the airfields that he put XXXXVIII Panzerkorps on alert to pull its 11. Panzer-Division out of the fighting along the Chir River and send it to Morozovskaya if Soviet armour continued to advance. He also directed Hoth – who was hard-pressed himself – to give up the 6. Panzer-Division to provide a mobile reserve for Heeresgruppe Don. Yet despite direction from von Richtofen to increase his security measures, Fiebig appears to have spent more time on the phone pleading with his superiors rather than doing what he could to protect his base. Kommando Flughafenbereich (Airbase Command) Koflug 4/XI was in charge of the airbase group at Tatsinskaya and it had a mixed anti-aircraft battalion (gemischte Flak-Abteilung 125) and a flak training unit, as well as Luftwaffe signal, supply and construction units available – perhaps 1,500–2,000 personnel excluding aircrew. In terms of weaponry, the Luftwaffe units initially had about a dozen 8.8cm flak guns and more than 40 2cm light flak guns in the vicinity of Tatsinskaya, but many were

LUFTWAFFE AIR UNITS AT TATSINSKAYA

The Luftwaffe air units stationed at Tatsinskaya were under the command of Generalleutnant Martin Fiebig's Fliegerkorps VIII, which was subordinate to Generaloberst Wolfram von Richtofen's Luftflotte 4. There were a total of eight transport *Gruppen* at the airbase, seven equipped with Ju-52 and one with Ju-86 transports, with a combined total of about 130 Ju-52 and 40 Ju-86 on the airfield at the time of the raid. There were also small detachments of Ju-88 bombers from I/KG 51 and Ju-88 reconnaissance planes from 3(F)/10. In addition, there were a number of damaged or non-operational aircraft at the airfield and the rail station, all of which were lost as well. The transport *Gruppen* were:

- K.Gr. z.b.v. 50 (Ju-52) Major Baumann
- K.Gr. z.b.v. 102 (Ju-52) Oberstleutnant Erdmann
- K.Gr. z.b.v. 105 (Ju-52) Major Jakobs
- K.Gr. z.b.v. 172 (Ju-52) Major Zähr
- K.Gr. z.b.v. 500 (Ju-52) Major Beckmann
- K.Gr. z.b.v. 700 (Ju-52)
- K.Gr. z.b.v. 900 (Ju-52) Oberst Wübben
- K.Gr. z.b.v. 22 (Ju-86)

24 DECEMBER 1942

0730hrs Badanov orders assault on Tatsinskaya

given to Gruppe Pfeiffer to reinforce its blocking detachments on the Bystraya River. Fiebig was left with only two 8.8cm and four 2cm flak guns to defend Tatsinskaya's perimeter. Due to the airlift, large quantities of ammunition were stored in dumps near the train station and even T35 anti-tank mines, but Fiebig did not consider using his construction troops to lay defensive minefields around the airfield.

In fact, Fiebig did virtually nothing to organize a ground defence – he appeared resigned to the loss of Tatsinskaya – nor did he increase the level of alertness. He spent much of the night of 23/24 December with his Fliegerkorps VIII staff in their command post inside the town of Tatsinskaya, but then finally decided to go to bed around 0500hrs. Apparently, many of the rest of his subordinates followed his example. When scouts from Badanov's 24th Tank Corps first approached the airfield before dawn on 24 December, they were surprised to find that the Luftwaffe flak positions were unmanned and that there were no real defences in place.

Fiebig's lack of leadership in the face of crisis stands in stark contrast to the attitude displayed by Oberstleutnant Georg Tyroller at the Kantemirovka-South airfield, who also came under attack from other elements of the 1st Guards Army on 23 December. Hastily organizing a ground defence with his flak troops, Tyroller knocked out 13 Soviet tanks and held the airfield even after it was surrounded. Eventually, the Luftwaffe was able to fly out Tyroller and his 1,957 men after an epic three-week stand. Unfortunately for the Luftwaffe, Fiebig was not cut from the same cloth as Tyroller.

24 DECEMBER 1942

0830hrs Nechayev's T-34s approach Tatsinskaya airfield

Thick fog near Tatsinskaya muffled the sound of the approaching Soviet tanks as Badanov's lead elements deployed for the raid. The town, which had a population of over 5,000 people, was quiet. After the unexpectedly determined resistance at Skosyrskaya, Badanov assumed that the Germans had fortified the town and decided in favour of a more deliberate approach instead of a *coup de main* against the airfield. His column had also spotted German vehicles moving on their eastern flank as they approached the town – they were part of Kampfgruppe Heinemann mounted on trucks – so

Badanov sent Lieutenant E. Morozova with a company of infantry, two tanks and two 76mm anti-tank guns to establish a blocking position so that these enemy troops could not interfere with the raid.

At 0730hrs, Badanov transmitted the signal '555' on his radio, causing the eight BM-13 launchers of the Guards Mortar Battalion to fire more than 100 132mm rockets into the town, setting part of it alight. The Fliegerkorps VIII command post was located in the town, and, by sheer luck, one of the rockets scored a direct hit on the telephone exchange building, severing Fiebig's link to Luftflotte 4 headquarters. Badanov hoped that the rocket barrage would cause any hidden German gun positions to reveal themselves, but there was no return fire. Nesterov's tankers began advancing as soon as the rocket bombardment began and by 0800hrs they had crossed the Tatsinskaya–Morozovskaya rail line. Nesterov sent his 1st Tank Battalion under Captain Ivan Linnik into the east side of the town in order to attack the train station, while committing the 2nd Tank Battalion under Captain Nechayev against the airfield.

As Nesterov's tankers advanced into Tatsinskaya, they caused many of the German support troops at the rail station to scatter and the Fliegerkorps VIII staff beat a hasty retreat to the airfield. Fiebig was awoken from two hours' sleep by the sound of rockets exploding nearby, which contributed to his deteriorating state of mind. He was hurriedly driven to the airfield, arriving around 0815hrs. Meanwhile, at the train station, Soviet tankers discovered a train with flatcars loaded with 50 damaged aircraft, intended for shipment back to repair depots in Germany, as well as a train loaded with aviation fuel. These trains, as well as the loading docks at the railyard, were soon set

24 DECEMBER 1942

0845hrs Fiebig orders all aircraft to take off immediately

The Luftwaffe had a few Flak 36 8.8cm guns at Tatsinskaya, which theoretically could have provided a perimeter anti-tank defence, at least until most aircraft could have taken off. Yet in reality, heavy fog on the morning of the raid greatly limited engagement ranges and the gun crews did not put up a spirited defence. (Ian Barter)

A 2cm flak position defending a Luftwaffe air base. Although the snow-block walls might afford some concealment to the gun crew, it offered no protection against tank attack. Tatsinskaya's flak units had little chance against even a company-size tank raid. (Bundesarchiv, Bild 101I-287-0872-03, Fotograf: Koll)

ablaze. Rather than German resistance in the town, the propensity of Soviet troops to loot captured German stores – particularly cigarettes, food and alcohol – inflicted delay as the Soviet tankers captured stockpiles near the rail yard. Soviet troops suffering from intense fatigue after a week on the steppe were quick to settle into the warm houses in the town. Civilians emerged to greet their liberators, inflicting further delay. Meanwhile, Nechayev's 2nd Battalion, with ten T-34s and ten T-70s, bypassed the town and headed south for the airfield. On the west side of Tatsinskaya, the 54th Tank Brigade began to engage some flak units on the north-west side of the town, but was not in a position to support the raid on the airfield immediately.

Even before Fiebig arrived on the base, the various group commanders had ordered all available aircrew to man their aircraft and start their engines in anticipation of an emergency evacuation. Many of the Ju-52s were still loaded with bulk supplies for Stalingrad, leaving little room for passengers. Frantic efforts were made to warm engines in order to start them, but there were only a limited number of engine-warming trucks available. Continuous flight operations in poor weather had reduced the operational readiness of most of the squadrons at Tatsinskaya to only 30–40 per cent, but on this frozen morning more than 100 of the estimated 180 aircraft made efforts to prepare for take-off. At best, Förster could load only about one-third of the Luftwaffe personnel on the base aboard transport aircraft, so he directed the remaining personnel to assemble near the southern perimeter of the base and prepare to flee in vehicles or even on foot. Kampfgruppe Philipp from the 306. Infanterie-Division was located 17km (10½ miles) to the south. Having given most of his available flak guns and personnel to von Heinemann, Fiebig had only a token force of 200 Luftwaffe personnel and six flak guns deployed to defend the base perimeter.

Arriving at the command bunker next to the control tower, Fiebig hesitated to order the emergency evacuation of Tatsinskaya without some kind of approval from higher headquarters, even though his communications with Luftflotte 4 were already disrupted by the Soviet raid. Fiebig gathered Förster and his eight transport *Gruppen* commanders in the command bunker, along with the Fliegerkorps VIII staff, where they watched him trying in vain to reach von Richtofen via HF radio. Oberst von Rohden was also present in the bunker as an observer, but failed to intervene in any way. A staff officer provided Fiebig with an updated weather report, which forecast extremely poor flying conditions, further weakening his resolve.

As the minutes ticked by, Nechayev's T-34s approached the north-east entrance of the airbase around 0830hrs. The 2cm flak battery located in revetments near the entrance briefly engaged Nechayev's tankers, but was quickly silenced. An 8.8cm battery was located on the north side of the base, but could not see the enemy due to the thick morning ground fog, which reduced visibility to fifty metres or less. Luftwaffe personnel could hear the sound of nearby explosions and machine-gun fire, but the fog made it difficult to determine exactly what was happening. Also, the noise produced by more than 300 engines revving on the flight line further obscured the proximity of the approaching threat. After a brief fight, Nechayev's tankers overran the 2cm battery and advanced onto the north-east corner of the airbase. In front of them, there were several wood-frame hangars, a number of large tents for the maintenance teams, stacks

Other Luftwaffe personnel man a machine-gun position equipped with a 7.92mm MG 15, which was a standard defensive weapon on Ju-52 transport aircraft. Despite the alert posture in this photo, most of Tatsinskaya's defensive positions were unmanned at the start of the raid. (Bundesarchiv, Bild 101I-394-1459-11, Fotograf: Wanderer)

THE TATSINSKAYA AIRFIELD RAID

DECEMBER 24, 1942

GERMAN POSITIONS

1 – 11

1 Parking aprons
2 Taxiways
3 Flight line
4 Guard post at main gate
5 2cm flak position, occupied
6 Maintenance hangers
7 Housing area
8 Tents
9 8.8cm flak position
10 Control tower
11 Fuel and ammuniton warehouses

EVENTS

1 Nechayev's Tank Battalion (2nd Bn, 130th Tank Brigade), attacking from the east.

2 A few tanks of the 54th Tank Brigade approach from the north-west in the final stages of the operation.

of spare engines and aircraft parts, fuel drums and rows of bombs. Beyond that, at the edge of visibility, was the bulk eight *Gruppen* of transport planes caught on the ground.

As Nechayev was fighting his way into the airfield, Major Lothar von Heinemann reached the north-west corner of the base in his *Kubelwagen* after bypassing Morozova's blocking detachment, and he headed straight to Fiebig's bunker. Von Heinemann had been shadowing Badanov's tankers since pulling out of Skosyrskaya, and once he deduced that the Soviet tanks were heading for Tatsinskaya, he gathered up some of his remaining truck-mounted troops and headed towards the airfield in the hope of warning Fiebig. Upon reaching the airfield, he witnessed Nechayev's tankers beginning to shell some parked aircraft on the runway and two transport planes exploding in balls of flame. Flight crew tumbled out of the burning aircraft, with their uniforms on fire. Von Heinemann realized that the airfield lacked any real defence against this enemy assault and he rushed into the bunker and reported to Fiebig that the base was being overrun by Soviet tanks, shouting, 'Herr General, you must take action! You must give permission to take off!'

Despite this shocking news, Fiebig still shrank from openly disobeying Hitler and Göring's direct orders – just as von Paulus was doing in Stalingrad by refusing to conduct an unauthorized breakout of AOK 6 – and lamely replied, 'For that I need Luftflotte authority, cancelling existing orders. In any case, it's impossible to take off in this fog.' Having just seen Soviet tanks advancing into the base, von Heinemann was in no mood for hair-splitting or prevarication, and he blurted out the obvious: 'Either you take that risk

A Kfz. 384 fuel truck refuels a Ju-52 transport. The presence of these trucks near the flight line made lucrative targets for Badanov's tankers and the loss of these specialized support vehicles was a severe setback to Fliegerkorps VIII. (Bundesarchiv, Bild 101I-330-3017-15A, Fotograf: Pfeiffer)

The flight line at Tatsinskaya was packed with nearly 200 transport aircraft on 24 December 1942. When the first Soviet shell landed a panic ensued as aircraft began trying to take off without coordination from the control tower, resulting in several collisions. (Bundesarchiv, Bild 101I-462-0953-07A, Fotograf: Heidrich)

or every unit on the airfield will be wiped out. All the transport units for Stalingrad, Herr General. The last hope of the surrounded 6. Armee!'

In the tight space of the bunker, Fiebig finally consented to do what he had desired all along. At about 0845hrs he gave all *Gruppen* commanders permission to take off immediately and told them to try to reach Novocherkassk, 80km (50 miles) to the south-west. As the commanders ran to their aircraft, Nechayev's tank crews were methodically destroying parked aircraft on the eastern end of the flight line. Yet due to the thick ground fog, the Soviet tankers could see only a portion of the transport fleet on the airbase.

When the first transport airplane on the parking apron took a hit from a 76mm high-explosive (HE) round, panic broke out on the flight line and there was little that the *Gruppen* commanders or the flight tower personnel could do to control the exodus. Snow was falling and thick fog lay over the entire airfield. Aircraft began taxiing and taking off from all over the airbase, with no priority but escape. Most aircraft converged into a fan shape, crowding towards take-off on the east end of the airfield. A number of aircraft damaged their wings or tails as they taxied into one another, rendering some unflyable. At first, some transport pilots tried to take off in small groups, but it quickly became chaos once Soviet T-34s were seen firing from one end of the runway. Two Ju-52 aircraft rose simultaneously into the air and collided with each other over mid-field, crashing in a heap of burning wreckage. Although Nechayev's tankers succeeded in destroying some operational aircraft, the bulk of the damage caused to the Luftwaffe aircraft was self-inflicted during the panicked mass take-off. At one point, Luftwaffe aircraft had to fly over the heads of Nechayev's tankers at the end of the runway, risking destruction from point-blank fire. The accuracy of the

SHUMATE
2011

The parking areas at Tatsinskaya were crowded with stacks of bombs and ammunition headed for Stalingrad. These boxes in the foreground hold rounds for 5cm PaK 38 anti-tank guns. (Author)

Russian tankers was not particularly good, and it is surprising how few transport planes were actually hit, although ammunition shortages played a role in limiting their firepower. In the later stages of the raid, some of Nechayev's T-34 tanks had apparently exhausted their main gun ammunition and they began ramming the tail sections of Ju-52 transports on the flight line, in order to prevent their take-off.

Within 30 minutes, most of the aircraft that could take off were gone and more Soviet troops were arriving on the airbase all the time. At least part of the 54th Tank Brigade began entering the north-west corner of the base in the last moments of the evacuation. Fiebig left his bunker shortly after 0900hrs and saw Soviet tanks driving into the base. The supply dump was on fire and burning wreckage littered the flight line. Oberstleutnant von Burgsdorf also arrived at the command bunker with a few of his troops and informed Fiebig that the Soviets had completely overrun the base and that 'there is absolutely no stopping them.' Fiebig, von Heinemann and the remaining Fliegerkorps VIII staff ran to a Ju-52 transport that had been held back for them. Feldwebel Ruppert was the pilot, but he had difficulty getting all three engines to start. Ruppert finally managed to take off under fire at 0915hrs, the last Luftwaffe plane to leave Tatsinskaya. Fiebig and his staff arrived at Rostov-West airfield an hour later and were immediately driven to Novocherkassk.

Amazingly, 108 Ju-52 transport planes and 16 Ju-86s were able to reach other German airfields, despite the atrocious flying weather and hasty take-

Many of the Soviet raiders were diverted from attacking the transports on the runway by the lure of the supply warehouses at Tatsinskaya, which held rations and ammunition. (Author)

off. One Ju-52 was successfully flown out by a Luftwaffe signals officer with no previous flying experience – a gifted amateur. However, at least 50 Luftwaffe aircraft were lost on the field, including 22 Ju-52s – mostly from Kampfgruppe (K.Gr.) z.b.v. 105, K.Gr. z.b.v. 500 and K.Gr. z.b.v. 700 – and 24 Ju-86 transports (from K.Gr. z.b.v. 22), two Ju-88 bombers (from I/KG 51) and two Ju-88 reconnaissance planes (from 3(F)/10). A vast store of supplies was captured at the base and in the town, including 300 tons of aviation fuel, three warehouses full of food and five warehouses of ammunition. There were also stocks of bombs and aviation spare parts at the airfield. In addition, all the fuel trucks and engine warming trucks were lost, which would make it difficult for Fliegerkorps VIII to continue the airlift from other airfields. Although German casualties in the raid are unknown, certainly dozens of Luftwaffe personnel were killed or wounded and perhaps 300–400 captured by Badanov's troops.

The actual number of Soviet troops who participated in the 30-minute raid on the airfield before Fiebig flew out at 0915hrs was not large – probably no more than 20 tanks and 50–60 infantrymen, which explains why so many German aircraft were able to escape. The bulk of Badanov's corps had become tangled up in clashes with rear-echelon troops around the town of Tatsinskaya and the German supply dumps. The 4th Guards Tank Brigade was engaged fighting a cluster of flak positions until 1100hrs and Badanov committed the 54th Tank Brigade to complete this action. Nevertheless, Soviet troops spent the bulk of the day mopping up German

THE T-70 LIGHT TANK

Since Soviet industry in 1942 still had difficulty producing enough T-34 medium tanks to outfit the new tank corps, some 40 per cent of the tanks in the 24th and 25th Tank Corps were the newly introduced T-70 light tanks. The Red Army was forced to use a mix of T-34s and T-70s to equip its armoured units, until production caught up with losses. Building light tanks allowed factories involved in truck or tractor production to switch quickly to constructing useful armoured vehicles, rather than the delay of waiting for medium tank production to increase. Previous Soviet light tanks, such as the T-40, T-50 and T-60, had proved disappointing in the 1941 campaigns, so a new design that was closer to medium tank qualities was sought.

The T-70 light tank was designed during the winter of 1941/42 and entered production in April 1942 at Plant No. 38 in Kirov and the GAZ plant in Gorkiy. In December 1942, Soviet industry built 710 T-70 tanks and 1,568 T-34s, which indicates the importance of the light tank programme in terms of fleshing out the new Soviet tank units. However, the T-70 was ill-suited for Deep Operations such as raids, because it lacked the mobility to keep up with the T-34 and it was intended primarily for infantry-support roles. Compared to the 30-ton T-34/76 Model 1943, the 9-ton T-70 had 23 per cent less operational range than its heavier cousin. Rather than a diesel engine as in the T-34, the T-70 was powered by two petrol-driven truck engines; this meant Soviet mixed tank battalions with T-34s and T-70s needed separate fuel trucks for each type of tank. While the 45mm main gun on the T-70 was sufficient to deal with enemy light tanks, it was inferior to the new long-barrelled models of German Pz III and Pz IV tanks. On the positive side, the T-70 had good armour for a light tank (the armour was sloped as in the T-34). Perhaps the greatest weakness of the T-70 was its two-man crew – only half that of the four-man crew of a T-34 – which was problematic both in combat and for daily maintenance requirements. The Red Army conceived of the T-70 as a scout tank, ranging ahead of the T-34 and complementing it with quantity, if not quality.

The use of the T-70 proved to be a liability in the Tatsinskaya raid since it lacked the mobility, endurance, firepower and durability of the T-34s. The handful of armoured cars in the tank corps had better mobility for reconnaissance and only the T-34 had the armament necessary to engage German Panzer units with any degree of success. In combat, the under-powered T-70s were likely to get stuck and the commander was overwhelmed with multiple tasks in his one-man turret. Although the Red Army continued to use light tanks in its tank corps as an expedient for a year after the raid, by early 1944 Soviet medium tank production had caught up to enable tank brigades to be outfitted entirely with T-34s.

troops inside Tatsinskaya, and Badanov did not consider the town secure until the evening. Badanov's command and control had been significantly reduced during the raid by the lack of sufficient radios and the thick fog. Rather than hitting Tatsinskaya airfield with a mailed fist, the Soviet tank corps had only struck a glancing blow, but it had been enough.

At 1700hrs, Badanov was able to gain radio contact by relay with Southwest Front headquarters and he reported: 'Tatsinskaya completely cleared of the enemy. 58 Tanks remaining: 39 T-34, 19 T-70. Provisions remaining: diesel fuel 0.2 [units], gasoline grade 1 2 [units], petrol 2nd grade 2 [units], ammunition 0.5 [units]. Corps has taken a defensive position. Infantry and tanks dug into the ground.'

Although Badanov had accomplished his mission, it was apparent that he had only a third of his armour remaining and that his supply state rendered the 24th Tank Corps virtually immobile. The T-34s were left with only 35–40 rounds each of 76mm ammunition and enough fuel to move about 50km (31 miles).

Ju-52s on the flight line at Tatsinskaya. The noise of more than 100 transport planes warming up for take-off drowned out the sound of Nechayev's approaching tanks. (Author)

While Badanov's troops were overrunning Tatsinskaya airfield, the Soviet plan to overrun the two Morozovskaya airfields was going awry. After capturing Milyutinskaya, Pavlov's tankers advanced cautiously towards Morozovskaya and then paused near the village of Uryupin on 24 December. But with his spearhead only 16km (10 miles) from their objective, the 25th Tank Corps was now virtually out of fuel and ammunition. Gruppe Spang was able to deploy new blocking forces in front of Pavlo, including Italians from the 2nd Mountain Division *Sforzesca*, while calling upon the Luftwaffe for help. Oberst Ernst Kuhl, in charge of the group of He-111 bombers being used as transports at Morozovskaya, had already evacuated all his aircraft to Novocherkassk upon Pavlov's approach and organized his flak teams to defend the base. Then he grimly hung on and waited for either von Manstein's promised reinforcements or a miracle to occur.

On Christmas morning, the miracle arrived in the form of clear skies over Morozovskaya. Realizing that Pavlov's tanks had come to a virtual standstill, Kuhl ordered some of his He-111 bombers and a dozen Stukas from I/St.G 2 to return and begin attacking the Soviet armoured column at Uryupin. Pavlov's tankers were caught stationary out on the open steppe with no cover, and the Luftwaffe bomber crews cut into them with a vengeance. With the Morozovskaya airfields almost within sight, the Stukas were able to take off, attack, return and re-arm very quickly. While the Stukas targeted the Soviet tanks, the He-111 bombers went after the softer fuel and ammunition trucks, blasting them to bits. After a day of relentless bombardment, Pavlov's 25th Tank Corps was reduced to only 25 operational tanks and he had little fuel left for manoeuvre. The 1st Guards Mechanized Corps still had some strength left, but it was involved in a protracted battle with Gruppe Spang's thin defensive line near Milyutinskaya, and was in no position to support a

Each Soviet T-34 carried about a half-dozen infantrymen, who dismounted as soon as the tank began to engage the enemy. The initial raiding party at Tatsinskaya was probably no more than 20 tanks and 60 infantrymen, which accounts for why more than three-quarters of the transport planes escaped. (RIA Novosti, 60231)

drive on Morozovskaya. Thus, the decimation of the 25th Tank Corps doomed the Soviet plan to seize Morozovskaya.

The German Reaction, 24 December

At first, the Germans had very little idea what had just hit Tatsinskaya or what the enemy situation was. After the bulk of Badanov's 24th Tank Corps had moved south from Skosyrskaya, most of the Gruppe Pfeiffer troops in the area re-formed and began to harass the 24th Motorized Rifle Brigade, which was still in the process of crossing the Bystraya. Kampfgruppe Tzschöckell, consisting mostly of *Nebel* (smoke) troops, was re-positioned to form a blocking force north of Tatsinskaya and to prevent the 24th Motorized Rifle Brigade and the remaining supply trucks from marching directly to Tatsinskaya.

In fact, the closest German combat unit was Gruppe Philipp, located 17km (10½ miles) south of Tatsinskaya at Nizhnekol'tsov. Gruppe Philipp was the last *Kampfgruppe* of the 306. Infanterie-Division en route to the front, and it consisted of Grenadier-Regiment 579, a flak battalion (three heavy and one light batteries), the divisional artillery trains and four StuG III assault guns from the 8. Luftwaffen-Feld-Division. Von Manstein ordered Gruppe Philipp to advance upon Tatsinskaya from the south and to support the impending counter-attack by XXXXVIII Panzerkorps. To the west of Tatsinskaya on the main rail line, Heeresgruppe Don stationed the armoured trains Panzerzug 10 and 28, plus a company of railway security police, to form another blocking detachment. These moves, however, were only made to contain Badanov's corps at Tatsinskaya and prevent it from causing

A number of German supply units were caught up in the raid and roughly handled by Badanov's tankers. However, many Soviet troops paused to loot captured stores, which aided Fiebig's escape with most of his transport crews. (Ian Barter)

further disruption to Heeresgruppe Don's lines of communication. Von Manstein intended to retake the airfield with XXXXVIII Panzerkorps and then encircle and destroy the Soviet raiding force, which based on the incoherent accounts from Fiebig's refugee pilots was initially thought to be only a brigade-size force.

At Tatsinskaya, once the ground fog cleared on the afternoon of 24 December a scene of burning desolation was revealed at the airfield. The exhausted but exultant Soviet soldiers joyfully looted captured German stores amidst still-smouldering wreckage. The post-adrenaline surge that often sets in after a successful raid now kicked in, and most of the Soviet troops were more focused on eating, getting drunk, warming up, sleeping or all of these, rather than consolidating a defensive position on the objective. Discipline was often a problem for the Red Army in the hour of victory, when troops became pre-occupied with personal inclinations and lost interest in follow-on missions.

Badanov had accomplished his mission, but now what? He still had irregular radio contact with Front headquarters and he was unaware whether or not Pavlov had succeeded with his raid on Morozovskaya. Unlike the typical centralized command and control in the Red Army, the nature of Deep Operations afforded Badanov an unusual amount of latitude in his decision-making. His first priority was to gather up his tank corps, which was scattered over a wide area, and to prevent his troops from slumbering into a post-raid funk that might make them useless for the next few days. The Soviet emphasis on combined-arms doctrine mandated that 24th Tank Corps should link up with Savchenko's motorized infantry as quickly as possible,

Wreckage littered Tatsinskaya airfield after the raid. Anticipating that they might withdraw, the raiders set most captured equipment and facilities ablaze, rendering the base unusable to the Luftwaffe when it returned four days after the raid. (Author)

since Badanov could not hold the town and airfield with a few companies of infantry. Badanov also desperately needed to find diesel fuel for his T-34s, but there was none in the captured German fuel stocks, which were primarily aviation-grade benzene.

After German resistance in Tatsinskaya was crushed, Badanov decided to send out scouts to determine where there were other enemy targets of opportunity as well as to improve his situational awareness. One platoon of armoured cars proceeded west along the main rail line, but soon came under fire from one of the armoured trains and stopped. Although armoured trains were vulnerable to heavy artillery and air attack, Badanov had neither, and thus this elderly weapon system trumped the light weaponry of his reconnaissance units. Another platoon of Soviet armoured cars followed the main rail line towards Morozovskaya and advanced 16km (10 miles) to Kovylkin Station before encountering any significant resistance. Badanov decided to reinforce this probe by sending Nechayev's battalion (ten T-34s and ten T-70 tanks) from the 130th Tank Brigade, some motorized infantry and his BM-13 multiple rocket launchers to advance north-east on Morozovskaya. His intention was to link up with Pavlov's forces, whom he expected to be in the area, and to keep his troops active.

Unknown to Badanov, his troops were moving into the approaching German dragnet. By the time that Tatsinskaya fell, the XXXXVIII Panzerkorps had dispatched the 11. Panzer-Division to an assembly area near Morozovskaya. Despite weeks of heavy fighting along the Chir River, General der Panzertruppen (General of Panzer Troops) Hermann Balck's 11. Panzer-Division was still a formidable fighting force, with about 70 per cent of its personnel, 66 tanks (19 Pz II, 43 Pz III and 4 Pz IV) and 25 artillery pieces. Unlike Badanov's tank corps, the 11. Panzer-Division was a balanced combined-arms force with its own artillery and sufficient fuel and ammunition to accomplish its missions. Balck was also a seasoned professional, with considerable experience in defeating Soviet tank groups.

Yet circumstances prevented Balck from using his entire division to crush the 24th Tank Corps at Tatsinskaya. He had to leave part of his division to cover Morozovskaya in case either the remnants of the 25th Tank Corps or 1st Mechanized Corps infiltrated through the thin German cordon. Balck was simultaneously tasked with restoring the screening force along the Bystraya River and crushing the Soviet raiding force at Tatsinskaya. He dispatched his most mobile troops, Kradschützen-Bataillon 61 (61st Motorcycle Infantry Battalion) and Panzer-Pionier-Bataillon 209 to Skosyrskaya, while sending a single tank battalion from Panzer-Regiment 15, all of Panzer-Grenadier-Regiment 111 and some mobile artillery to advance upon Tatsinskaya. At his Wolfsschanze headquarters in East Prussia, Hitler was enraged to hear about the capture of Tatsinskaya and ordered that the 24th Tank Corps should be immediately crushed and that no prisoners should be taken. Under pressure from Hitler to expedite the riposte, von Manstein decided to also send Kampfgruppe Unrein from the 6. Panzer-Division to assist Balck at Tatsinskaya.

Late on 24 December, Balck's Panzer troops bumped into the 130th Tank Brigade in a meeting engagement near the village of Babovnya. A deep *balka* (ravine) slowed the Soviet advance and they were engaged by Panzer-Regiment 15 as they were negotiating their way through the obstacle. An

Soviet T-34 crewmen in the winter of 1942/43. By the time that Badanov's corps reached Tatsinskaya, his tanks were low on fuel and his men exhausted after a six-day approach march. (Author)

Two German armoured trains helped to prevent Badanov's reconnaissance troops from pushing westward along the main rail line and destroying more of the train stations. Badanov's inability to handle the armoured trains indicates the weakness of the air and artillery support available to his tank corps in the Deep Operation mission. (Nik Cornish, WH 648)

hour-long tank battle developed and ultimately seven Soviet tanks were knocked out before Nesterov ordered his troops to pull back. Five German tanks were also disabled, but were eventually recovered. A Ukrainian tank officer, Lieutenant Aleksei I. Daniltschenko, was captured from one of the abandoned Soviet tanks and he revealed the size and composition of the 24th Tank Corps to his interrogators.

As night fell, the Soviets withdrew from Kovylkin Station and assumed a defensive hedgehog formation near Point 175, 5 kms north-east of Tatsinskaya. The 11. Panzer-Division elements formed a screen three kms from them and awaited reinforcements. At Skosyrskaya, the *Kradschützen-Bataillon* re-occupied the town and emplaced a 75-mm PaK anti-tank gun covering the bridge. Many of the damaged Soviet tanks and other vehicles in the town were abandoned when Savchenko retreated. By Christmas Eve, both Balck and Badanov knew that the 24th Tank Corps was now isolated.

24 DECEMBER 1942

0915hrs Fiebig evacuated from Tatsinskaya

Last Stand, 25–27 December

On Christmas day, Badanov moved his headquarters into some buildings on the northern edge of Tatsinskaya, where he was concentrating his defence. With most of Savchenko's 24th Motorized Rifle Brigade still at Skosyrskaya, Badanov had barely 50 tanks and about 2,000 troops concentrated around Tatsinskaya, which were insufficient resources to hold the town and the airfield. Realizing that a German counter-attack was developing, Badanov formed his three available brigades into hedgehog positions on the north side of the town of Tatsinskaya, at D'yakonov and Talovskiy. With most of his fuel gone, Badanov decided to hunker down around the town and await rescue by the approaching 3rd Guards Army, to which he was now subordinate.

Badanov's exhausted troops settled into the town, devouring captured German food stocks and clearing skulking German troops out of basements and other hiding places. A special NKVD detachment led by an officer named Andreev assisted in hunting down Germans, as well as trying to identify Soviet civilians in the town who had collaborated with the enemy. As many citizens would discover, the arrival of the Red Army could be a two-edged sword, with liberation for some and persecution for others.

Meanwhile, Savchenko made a renewed daylight effort to push through the German screening forces near Skosyrskaya and succeeded in reaching the villages of Oblivskiy and Kryukov before being stopped. Yet as more reinforcements arrived from the 11. Panzer-Division, Gruppe Pfeiffer's resistance stiffened. Savchenko's brigade was also running low on fuel and ammunition. Unable to get his entire brigade through to Tatsinskaya, Savchenko decided to wait for dark and then try and infiltrate several small groups through gaps in Gruppe Pfeiffer's screen.

On the afternoon of Christmas Day, Panzer-Regiment 15 from the 11. Panzer-Division began probing attacks against the Soviets in D'yakonov and succeeded in knocking out another four tanks, but suffered 36 personnel casualties of its own. Communications between Badanov and Vatutin improved somewhat now that his signal team could employ radio-teletype from a fixed site, although coordination was still sluggish. At 1800hrs, Badanov sent a message to Southwest Front requesting immediate assistance. Vatutin informed him that 25th Tank Corps and 1st Mechanized Corps were en route, but in fact these units were over 40km (25 miles) away and badly depleted.

Around 0500hrs on 26 December, five T-34 tanks and three fuel trucks from Savchenko's brigade managed to slip through German lines and reach Badanov's corps at Tatsinskaya. An hour later, another small group arrived,

After his success at Tatsinskaya, Badanov sent the 130th Tank Brigade and some infantry towards Morozovskaya, hoping to link up with Pavlov's 25th Tank Corps. Instead, they ran straight into the 11. Panzer-Division, dispatched to deal with the raiders. (RIA Novosti, 42340)

A battalion of Pz III tanks from Panzer-Regiment 15/11. Panzer-Division were the first substantial reinforcements to arrive near Tatsinskaya on the afternoon of 24 December. Note how the tanks use peasant *izbas* (houses) for concealment. (Ian Barter)

but that was it. Savchenko could provide no further assistance to Badanov's trapped forces. Around 0730hrs, Badanov received a radio message from Vatutin that stated: 'The corps is transformed into a Guards unit. You were awarded the Order of Suvorov, 2nd degree. I congratulate you and the entire staff of the corps and wish you victory over the enemy.'

It was apparent that Vatutin did not appreciate the 24th Tank Corps' dangerous situation. Badanov was less impressed with titles and medals, and pressed Vatutin for immediate assistance. 'The corps is experiencing an acute shortage of ammunition. A substitute for diesel fuel is being prepared. I beg you to provide air cover and accelerate the advance of army units. I beg you to commence aviation bombardment [of the enemy].'

Yet when the sun came up, it was the Luftwaffe and not the VVS that appeared over Tatsinskaya. German reconnaissance aircraft began flying over the town and methodically identified most of Badanov's positions. No Soviet fighters appeared to interfere with them. Once they were satisfied that they had detected most of the 24th Tank Corps elements around Tatsinskaya, the Luftwaffe returned in late morning with Ju-87 dive-bombers and He-111 level bombers to pulverize the town and the airfield. The town was bombed mercilessly and significant losses were inflicted on both Badanov's soldiers and the local civilian population. Badanov's anti-aircraft units proved unable to protect the corps in its dispersed defensive positions and failed to shoot down any German aircraft. Then while the Soviet defenders were still stunned, Balck sent in a mixed Kampfgruppe of tanks and Panzergrenadiers towards the east side of the airfield. Badanov was caught by surprise, since he had only three tanks from the 54th Tank Brigade and some infantry guarding the airfield, while the bulk of his forces defended the northern edge of the town. Since most of his tanks were reduced to immobilized pillboxes due to fuel shortages, his mobile reserve was reduced to five T-34s led by Captain Nechayev. Badanov ordered Nechayev to defeat the German armoured probe towards the airfield.

Nechayev's T-34s advanced southward into the flank of the oncoming German *Kampfgruppe*, which had about a company of Pz III tanks and some Panzerjägers. A long-range gunnery duel began and continued for more than an hour, with vehicles using peasant *izbas* (houses) for concealment. Eventually, all five Soviet T-34s were burning and Nechayev was dead. Although most Soviet-era accounts claim that a wounded Nechayev heroically rammed his burning T-34 tank into a German tank, there is no indication that the Germans suffered any significant losses in this action. The 11. Panzer-Division suffered three killed and 17 wounded on 26 December, but any tanks damaged in the action were recovered and repaired. Nechayev's counter-attack had delayed the German attack, but the Germans still gained positions within sight of the airfield. Most of Badanov's remaining tank ammunition was consumed in this action and he knew that his defence could not hold out much longer. Due to irregular radio communications with Lelyushenko and Vatutin, Badanov decided to send a liaison officer in an armoured car to infiltrate through German lines in order to emphasize the desperate plight of the 24th Tank Corps with higher command. Miraculously, this officer managed to slip through the encirclement and reach Lelyushenko's headquarters, but his report made little difference.

At 2200hrs, Badanov was able to get through to Vatutin and reported: 'Situation critical. No tanks. Large losses of personnel. Have lost half my officers. Cannot keep Tatsinskaya. I ask permission to withdraw from the area. Enemy transport aircraft on the airfield are destroyed.' Amazingly, Badanov's request to evacuate Tatsinskaya was refused. Even though the

Unlike Badanov's corps, Balck's 11. Panzer-Division deployed as a combined-arms team, with its own artillery regiment. Balck's division had 25 artillery pieces and five 8.8cm flak guns to throw into the fight at Tatsinskaya. (Ian Barter)

EVENTS

1. 24 December 1942: Badanov sends a reinforced tank battalion from the 130th Tank Brigade to link up with the 25th Tank Corps, but it bumps into the approaching 11. Panzer-Division and fights a tank battle at Kovylkin Station and near Lugovoy.
2. A Soviet reconnaissance west along the rail line is repulsed by a German armored train.
3. Von Manstein orders Kampfgruppe Philipp to advance toward Tatsinskaya and form a blocking position to the south of the airfield.
4. Balck sends two battalions from 11. Panzer-Division to reinforce KG Heinemann at Skosyrskaya.
5. 25 December 1942: Badanov pulls his three tank brigades into a tight defensive perimeter around the town of Tatsinskaya and awaits relief.
6. Colonel Savchenko makes several attempts to push through to reach Badanov but only a few small groups succeed. German reinforcements eventually push his weakened 24th Motorized Rifle Brigade out of Skosyrskaya and across the Bystraya.
7. The battered 25th Tank Corps is virtually immobilized north of Uryupin due to fuel and ammunition shortages and unable to aid Badanov's forces.
8. 26 December 1942: 11. Panzer-Division occupies strong blocking positions north and east of the town while the Luftwaffe bombs the 24th Tank Corps. Then 11. Panzer-Division attacks toward the airfield.
9. 27 December 1942: A Kampfgruppe from 6. Panzer-Division arrives to form blocking positions on the west side of the town, while German air and artillery attacks on 24th Tank Corps intensify. Badanov's position is becoming desperate.
10. 28 December 1942: Badanov conducts a breakout operation through a gap in the German perimeter and succeeds in reaching Mikhaylov and eventually reaching approaching 3rd Guards Army units north of the Bystraya.

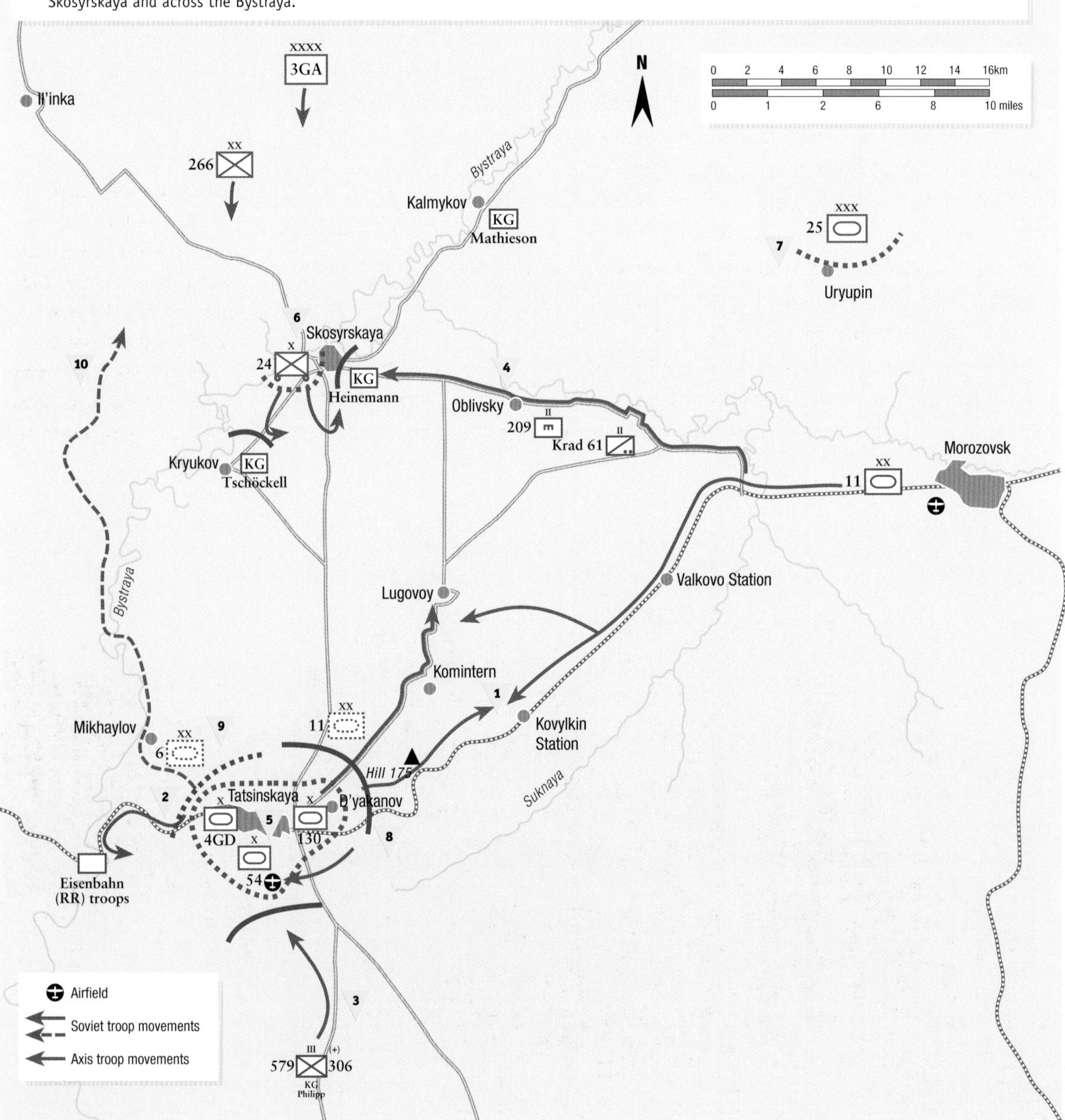

Isolation and Infiltration

operation was conceived as a raid, Stalin no longer wanted to give up the airfield since he recognized that holding it had great propaganda value. Instead, he personally ordered Vatutin to make every effort to save the 24th Tank Corps, but that the airfield was to be held. In a telephone conference, Stalin told Vatutin that 'your prime task is to prevent destruction of Badanov's corps and relieve him with Pavlov and Russiyanov [Lieutenant-General Russiyaniv, 1st Guards Mechanized Corps] as soon as you can.' Soon afterwards, Stalin again signalled Vatutin and reminded him to 'keep Badanov in mind all the time. Rescue him in any case.'

25–27 DECEMBER 1942

24th Tank Corps holds out in Tatsinskaya against German attacks

Vatutin informed Stalin about Badanov's request to withdraw from Tatsinskaya, stating: 'I demanded Badanov to hold on to Tatsinskaya but at the same time told him he could reach another decision only in the most extreme circumstances. It is possible I was mistaken on this, but I believe in Badanov and will encourage him constantly.' Clearly, Vatutin wanted to duck the tough decision here and leave it up to either Stalin to condemn the 24th Tank Corps to a hopeless last stand or Badanov to disobey orders and abandon his post. Stalin and Zhukov, conversing with Vatutin, commented that 'You have acted correctly in allowing Badanov to abandon Tatsinskaya in the most extreme conditions.' Stalin's instructions about Tatsinskaya were amazingly similar to Hitler's instructions to Fiebig about holding the airfield – withdrawal would be regarded as permissible only once enemy tanks were overrunning the position.

By 26 December, Lelyushenko's 3rd Guards Army was the closest Soviet formation to Tatsinskaya, but was still about 65km (40 miles) north of the town. Pavlov's 25th Tank Corps and Russiyanov's 1st Guards Mechanized

Panzergrenadiers from 11. Panzer-Division ride a Pz III tank during mop-up operations against the 24th and 25th Tank Corps. Balck quickly stationed small groups of tanks and infantry around Tatsinskaya to isolate Badanov's corps. (Ian Barter)

Unable to reach Morozovskaya, Badanov deployed his remaining tanks in defensive positions around the town of Tatsinskaya and the airbase. However, the tanks were virtually immobilized from lack of fuel and had little ammunition left. (Nik Cornish, K9)

Corps were somewhat closer, but their combat power was virtually spent. Nevertheless, at 0505hrs on 27 December, Vatutin ordered Lelyushenko to force march the 25th Tank Corps and 1st Guards Mechanized Corps to link up with Badanov's encircled corps as soon as possible and 'destroy the enemy in the Tatsinskaya region.' Badanov was ordered to sit tight and told that his corps had priority for replacements and as soon as it was relieved it would be given a follow-on pursuit mission. Unfortunately, Vatutin's orders not only ignored the battered condition of these three mechanized units, but also that German resistance was stiffening north of Tatsinskaya and Morozovskaya, as Armee Abteilung Hollidt's improvised *Kampfgruppen* were finally able to establish a near-continuous front. Despite Stalin's insistence, Badanov's prospects for immediate rescue appeared remote.

Throughout 26 December, additional German forces were arriving around Tatsinskaya, and Balck would soon have the means to crush Badanov's command. Another *Kampfgruppe* from 6. Panzer-Division, comprising some tanks and the SPWs of the II. Bataillon, Panzer-Grenadier Regiment 114, arrived to bolster the 11. Panzer-Division. Gruppe Philipp also closed up on the airfield from the south, further strengthening the noose around Badanov. By the evening of 26 December, the Germans had parts of two Panzer divisions and a reinforced infantry regiment surrounding Tatsinskaya, although there were still a few gaps on the west side of the town. Due to Stalin's involvement,

Vatutin knew that he had to appear to be making every effort to save Badanov's corps, even though he probably recognized that the Germans would crush 24th Tank Corps long before a rescue force arrived. The truth in Isserson's doctrine about the necessity of pulling a mechanized corps back to refit after a successful raid was quietly ignored.

Although Lelyushenko's 3rd Guards Army tried to batter its way through to Badanov on 27 December, Armee Abteilung Hollidt's makeshift defences held. After 12 days of advancing and attacking, Operation *Little Saturn* was fast approaching its culminating point, where Vatutin's offensive capabilities no longer exceeded Hollidt's defensive strength. Radio communications between Badanov and Vatutin were still irregular, except in the evening hours. In order to determine Badanov's situation more fully, the Southwest Front dispatched two different Po-2 liaison aircraft to reach Tatsinskaya airfield – one of them was shot down by the Luftwaffe and the other landed intact behind 11. Panzer-Division lines near Komintern. The captured aircraft and pilot revealed that Badanov was isolated and had only irregular contact with his higher headquarters. German radio intercepts also revealed that Badanov was perilously low on fuel and ammunition and that he was grimly hanging on for rescue.

By 27 December, Balck had sufficient combat power to launch concentric attacks on Badanov's trapped corps and he began by using his divisional

When the weather finally cleared on Christmas Day, the Stukas from I/St.G 2 based at Morozovskaya had a field day against Pavlov's exposed 25th Tank Corps. Badanov's corps also lost a number of vehicles to air attack, and the failure of the VVS to provide any kind of air cover to the raiding force was a bitter blow to the Soviet force. (Bundesarchiv, Bild 101I-329-2984-05A, Fotograf: Weber, Willi)

artillery to pound the town. Badanov's multiple rocket launchers were now out of ammunition and his few available mortars lacked the range to compete with 10cm and 15cm howitzers. The Luftwaffe also returned and methodically reduced the town to a splintered wreck with a series of intense bombardments. Badanov's anti-aircraft batteries had too little ammunition left to oppose the Luftwaffe seriously, and the German aircraft now owned the skies over Tatsinskaya.

After receiving little return fire, the 11. Panzer-Division mounted a successful afternoon attack on the 130th Tank Brigade's defensive position at D'yakonov and was able to occupy this village by nightfall. Almost out of ammunition, Nesterov's troops had to fall back. Simultaneously, the 6. Panzer-Division mounted a combined-arms attack with 16 tanks and a battalion of Panzergrenadiers against the 54th Tank Brigade positions on the west side of Tatsinskaya. Badanov had only a few tanks left and he committed them to hold his shrinking perimeter, but fuel and ammunition shortages limited his armour's ability to respond to the German attacks. In desperation, Badanov ordered his troops to use captured German weapons, including a PaK gun or two, and some flak guns. Assisted by his last battery of 76mm guns, Badanov's troops managed to prevent the Germans from overrunning the entire perimeter, but by the end of the day there was no main gun ammunition left for the tanks.

The Soviet Southwest Front sent two PO-2 biplanes to re-establish communications with Badanov's corps, but one was shot down and the other landed behind German lines and was captured. The failure toplan adequately for maintaining long-distance communications provided one of the major lessons about Deep Operations during the raid. (Bundesarchiv, Bild 169-0112, Fotograf: Zwimer)

After the raid, burnt-out tanks and vehicles litter the area between Tatsinskaya and the Bystraya River. Most of Badanov's T-34s had run out of fuel by the time that the German counter-attack began in earnest and were easily shot up. (Nik Cornish, WH 636)

After the loss of D'yakonov, Badanov knew that he could not repulse another one of Balck's attacks. Fortuitously, Badanov's radio operators were finally able to establish reliable contact with Lelyushenko's approaching 3rd Guards Army, and they relayed traffic to Vatutin's Southwest Front headquarters. Badanov again requested permission to withdraw. Here Soviet post-war efforts to 'correct' history muddy the waters. According to post-war accounts by Zhukov (who was in Moscow), Vatutin authorized Badanov to begin a breakout operation as soon as possible. However, based upon how Badanov was later treated and the fact that Stalin had mandated that Tatsinskaya be held, it is likely that Vatutin continued to turn down Badanov's request. Apparently, Badanov was told to hold because relief was on the way. Even the awarding of the Guards title to the corps and the Order of Suvorov to Badanov appears very much a gesture to men who were already written off by the Southwest Front.

Exfiltration, 28 December

28 DECEMBER 1942

0300hrs Badanov leads breakout from Tatsinskaya

Whether authorized or not, Badanov began to make preparations for a withdrawal after surviving the German onslaught on 27 December. Two major problems faced him. Firstly, there was no diesel fuel left for the T-34 tanks and it would be very difficult to break through the German encirclement without them. Secondly, hundreds of Badanov's men were wounded and huddling in the cellars in Tatsinskaya to avoid the bombardment – it would be nigh on impossible to remove these men. Badanov also realized that he would need some kind of diversion in order to facilitate his breakout, given that the Germans had observation on the town from all angles.

Colonel V. Orlova, the assistant corps commander and an engineer, solved the first problem by devising a substitute for diesel fuel by mixing one part gasoline with three parts captured German B-4 (87 octane) aviation fuel, along with some benzene. Although the resulting mix could be run in the T-34's diesel engine, it would inevitably damage the fuel-injection system after even short usage and eventually cause the vehicle to stop. Badanov ordered the fuel mixture to be put into the few remaining T-34 tanks, which he intended to use to lead the breakout. Vatutin made another gesture to Badanov after dusk on 27 December, when 14 Soviet Li-2 (license-built DC-3) transports overflew the airfield and dropped supplies by parachute. All told, the Li-2s dropped 3.2 tons of gasoline, 1.2 tons of diesel fuel, 535 boxes of 76mm shells, 750 boxes of 45mm shells, 18,000 rifle rounds and 560 boxes of hand grenades. However the accuracy of the airdrop was poor and less than half the canisters fell within Badanov's position. The amount of supplies recovered was only sufficient to restock a single tank company, the anti-tank batteries and some of the remaining motorized infantry. No effort was made by Soviet aircraft to land on the captured runway to either evacuate Badanov's wounded or to unload bulk fuel or tank ammunition. Clearly, Southwest Front had written off the 24th Tank Corps.

Badanov called a council of war with his remaining officers at 2200hrs. Despite heavy losses, all three tank brigade commanders and his chief of staff were still functional. After brief discussion, he decided that the remaining combat-worthy troops of the 24th Tank Corps would begin a breakout within four hours. All of the wounded would be left behind, even though he was probably aware that Hitler had issued a 'no prisoners' decree

By mixing captured German aviation fuel with other petroleum and oil products, Badanov's chief engineer was able to get a few tanks running. Crowding as many men as possible onto the remaining vehicles, Badanov conducted a breakout operation early on the morning of 28 December and reached Soviet lines with the survivors. (Nik Cornish, T35)

Although Badanov escaped back to Soviet lines, many of his troops were left behind and eventually captured or killed by 11. Panzer-Division. Here, German infantry round up warmly dressed Russians from underneath a railroad crossing. (Ian Barter)

with regard to his men. Badanov also said that a diversion would be necessary in order for the breakout to succeed, and a team of 300 'volunteers' was designated to fill that role.

Badanov knew that his only chance for escape lay on the poorly guarded west side of the German encirclement. The Germans had just moved in Panzer-Grenadier Regiment 4 from 6. Panzer-Division to cover this sector, but there were gaps between its positions and those of Panzer-Regiment 15. Around 0200hrs on 28 December, Badanov directed his diversionary force to simulate a breakout towards the north-east. As the Germans reacted to this activity, Badanov began his breakout with the main body on the west side of town at 0300hrs. Badanov led the column, which had 11 tanks and 30 trucks, as well as 927 of his men. Thanks to the diversionary force, Badanov's column initially slipped through the gap between the Panzergrenadiers and the Panzer unit without being noticed. Eventually, the column was spotted and the Germans knocked out two tanks, but could not prevent the escape of the rest of the column into the gloomy winter night. Badanov headed his column north-west towards Mikhaylov and the approaching units of the 3rd Guards Army. No member of Badanov's diversionary force escaped the German encirclement and none were ever given any awards or recognition.

On the morning of 28 December, elements of 11. Panzer-Division moved into the deserted Tatsinskaya airfield, which was briefly re-occupied by the

SHUMATE
2011

Luftwaffe, but Fliegerkorps VIII was unwilling to resume transport operations from the devastated base. According to some German accounts, the mutilated bodies of Luftwaffe personnel captured during the initial raid were found by Balck's troops, but this may have been an effort to conceal German war crimes at Tatsinskaya. Several hundred Soviet wounded were captured in the town and given Hitler's no-prisoner order, it is likely that all were dealt with summarily as there is no mention of interrogations in 11. Panzer-Division records. Three days later, the Germans abandoned Tatsinskaya for good, as troops from 3rd Guards Army approached.

After a day-long trek through the snow, with many troops reduced to walking, the survivors of 24th Tank Corps made it through to the 266th Rifle Division of the 3rd Guards Army on the Bystraya. Badanov's corps – now the 2nd Guards Tank Corps *Tatsinskaya* – was so badly depleted that even when the separated 24th Motorized Rifle Brigade rejoined its ranks, it barely had one-third of its authorized strength in personnel and less than 10 per cent of its tanks and vehicles. Normally, Soviet doctrine was to pull a badly depleted tank corps back into Stavka reserve to rebuild, but apparently the Soviet High Command was none too pleased with Badanov's unauthorized withdrawal. Instead, Vatutin put him in nominal command of the remnants of his corps, plus the burnt-out wrecks of the 25th Tank Corps and the 1st Guards Mechanized Corps and told him that it was his responsibility to lead the advance across the Bystraya and retake Tatsinskaya. Altogether, these three units had barely 50 tanks and very little infantry left, which meant assigning them an offensive mission was intended more as punishment than as a realistic operation. However, Badanov's semi-mechanized group was only lightly involved in the final 3rd Guards Army push across the Bystraya before the Stavka abruptly ended *Little Saturn* on

German troops unload supplies from a Ju-52 during the Stalingrad airlift. (Ian Barter)

The 6. Panzer-Division also dispatched a reinforced *Kampfgruppe* to deal with Badanov's raid. (Ian Barter)

30 December. Heeresgruppe Don had survived the Soviet offensive – just barely – and now Vatutin's entire command needed refitting before it could renew its advance.

Badanov's 2nd Guards Tank Corps was finally withdrawn to rebuild, but it took nearly six months until it was combat-ready again, and it did not see action again until the Battle of Kursk in July 1943. Pavlov's 25th Tank Corps failed to reach its objective in the raid, but was not as badly depleted as Badanov's outfit. After a brief refit in January 1943, Pavlov's corps was recommitted on 15 February to join Vatutin's Operation *Gallop* offensive towards the Dnepr River. Once again, Pavlov's corps found itself advancing in a spearhead role, and although it almost reached the city of Dnepropetrovsk, it was soon exposed and vulnerable. With his tanks running out of fuel once again, Pavlov found himself in the path of von Manstein's 'Backhand Blow' counter-offensive and his corps was virtually annihilated and he was captured. A new 25th Tank Corps was rebuilt by late 1943 with a sprinkling of survivors, but Pavlov's corps had the dubious distinction of being involved in two failed Deep Operations.

Heeresgruppe Don had deployed several German infantry divisions to strengthen the Italian 8th Army sector on the Don, and these units put up fierce resistance before withdrawing. (Ian Barter)

Generalleutnant Martin Fiebig survived his role in the debacle at Tatsinskaya and was given other commands after Stalingrad. After the war, however, he was found guilty of war crimes by the Government of Yugoslavia and executed in 1947. Hermann Balck rose quickly over the two years after the raid from command of 11. Panzer-Division to a Panzerkorps, then Panzerarmee and finally Heeresgruppe G in Alsace. Yet his star was fading even before the end of the war, and he was later convicted of criminal actions and did not serve in the Bundeswehr. Georg Pfeiffer, whose steadfast leadership helped to stabilize the situation around Tatsinskaya, continued to be a pillar of strength in the Wehrmacht until he was killed in action as a corps commander during Operation *Bagration* in June 1944. Georgiy Isserson was released from prison in 1951, and although he tried to retrieve his reputation, his contributions to Soviet Deep Operations theory were swept under the rug until well after the collapse of the Soviet Union.

ANALYSIS

The Soviet Deep Operation against Tatsinskaya airfield succeeded in reaching its objective and inflicting serious losses of material on the Luftwaffe. During 24–26 December, the Luftwaffe airlift to Stalingrad was temporarily suspended as a direct result of the raid. While the failure of the ground rescue operation, *Wintergewitter*, to reach Stalingrad in December was serious, it did not spell immediate doom for the encircled AOK 6, since Hitler was intent upon transferring two Panzer divisions from Heeresgruppe A in the Caucasus and making a renewed effort in January or February 1943. However, the overall failure of the Luftwaffe airlift – exacerbated by the loss of Tatsinskaya airfield – demonstrated that AOK 6 could not be kept alive until rescue arrived. The Luftwaffe's attempts to restart the airlift after the raid from safer airfields such as Ssalsk, greatly increased the distance to Stalingrad and caused the already meagre airlift effort to collapse. The loss of Tatsinskaya and Morozovskaya airfields, as well as the threat to Heeresgruppe Don's main lines of communication between Rostov and Tormosin, were the final straws that demolished any hope of saving AOK 6. If the Soviet raids had failed to reach either objective, then AOK 6 would still have been overwhelmed but probably at a much greater cost in time and casualties to the Red Army.

The raid on Tatsinskaya was the first successful Deep Operation conducted to depths beyond 100km (62 miles) by Soviet mechanized forces, but it revealed a number of problems that had not been discovered in pre-war manoeuvres. Command and control was particularly problematic, given both the Soviet aversion to using radios due to fear of interception and the limited number of suitable long-distance radios at corps level. Once Badanov moved off into the void, his corps had irregular communication with higher headquarters for nearly a week. Poor communication with Southwest Front also meant that Badanov hit the objective fairly blind, with no recent intelligence updates from Soviet reconnaissance flights or knowledge of German activity in the area.

Weak logistical capabilities in the tank corps was another key deficiency revealed by the raid. Although the T-34 tank was designed to go long

Generalmajor Hermann Balck, commander of the 11. Panzer-Division. Balck was an experienced Panzer commander and a formidable opponent for Badanov. (Bundesarchiv Bild 101I-732-0118-03, Fotograf: Bauer)

distances over open steppe in winter conditions, the six-day march from the Don River bridgehead to Tatsinskaya was brutal on the trucks in 24th Tank Corps, causing a high rate of loss from mechanical failure. Every truck lost en route meant less fuel and ammunition being carried, and more fuel was consumed during the journey than expected. By the time Badanov reached his objective, his tanks had only a 0.2 fuel load left and 0.5 load of ammunition, and this was quickly expended fighting 11. Panzer-Division. This situation begs the question: why did Southwest Front not plan for an airlift of diesel fuel and ammunition into Tatsinskaya once Badanov secured the airfield? The 17th Aviation Army had at least 14 Li-2 transport planes available, but these were not employed to support Badanov until his situation was hopeless. For that matter, the raiding force could have moved much more quickly to the objective if it could have received daily fuel drops from the VVS, thereby reducing the need to bring so many supply trucks along. Vatutin's failure to provide any kind of fighter cover of Badanov's encircled corps was inexcusable and baffling.

All of these deficiencies in Soviet air–ground coordination highlight an aspect of combined-arms warfare that the Germans had learned in 1939–40 but which the Red Army was still learning – air support, artillery, mobile infantry, reliable communications and logistics are just as essential ingredients for success as tanks. During the Tatsinskaya raid, only one side demonstrated effective air–ground coordination and that was Fliegerkorps VIII and XXXXVIII Panzerkorps. Although the Red Army had created tank corps in emulation of the Panzer divisions, it had yet to replicate and understand all the components needed for the successful conduct of Deep Operations.

Soviet intelligence support provided to Badanov's corps was also inadequate to conduct this kind of raid properly. In addition to missing the arrival of 306. Infanterie-Division in the vicinity of the two airfields, and Gruppe Pfeiffer's screening forces on the Bystraya River line, Badanov was not provided with regular updates on the location of Heeresgruppe Don's Panzer divisions. In fact, the raiding force was highly dependent upon acquiring geographic information from local civilians throughout the operation.

In terms of battle command, Badanov lost tight control over his 24th Tank Corps in the final leg of the march to the objective, which resulted in his corps splitting apart at Skosyrskaya and reaching Tatsinskaya in dribs and drabs, rather than as a consolidated mass of armour. One can imagine what would have happened to Fiebig's transport force if Badanov had reached the airfield with over 100 tanks instead of 20. The fact that the Luftwaffe lost only about a third of its aircraft at Tatsinskaya demonstrates that the Soviet armoured spearhead was too strung out by the time that it reached its objective. Adverse weather also had a huge impact on the outcome of the raid, enabling the Soviets to get within striking range without being noticed, but then adding confusion at the objective due to heavy fog. Badanov missed the opportunity to eliminate the entire Fliegerkorps VIII

After losing Tatsinskaya, the Luftwaffe airlift rapidly dwindled. Eventually it was only possible to supply the 6. Armee by air drop, which was clearly inadequate. (Nik Cornish, WH 655)

staff at Tatsinskaya, which would have further crippled Luftwaffe air operations at a critical moment.

As a result of the difficulty in coordinating three different tank and mechanized corps during this Deep Operation, the Stavka concluded that an even larger tank formation than the tank corps was required to successfully conduct manoeuvres into the depth of enemy defences. This conclusion spurred the creation of tank armies, which appeared only two months after the raid as the Popov Mobile Group in Operation *Gallop*. Even Pavlov's 25th Tank Corps, partly rebuilt after the Morozovskaya Raid, became part of the Popov Mobile Group and spearheaded the drive towards the Dnepr River. At one point, Pavlov's tankers were only 32km (20 miles) from Adolf Hitler, who had flown in to Zaporozhe to consult with von Manstein before hurriedly leaving when he learned how close Soviet armour had approached. Unfortunately, the Popov Group was little more than a loosely coordinated group of individual tank corps rather than a cohesive tank army, which enabled von Manstein to outmanoeuvre it and defeat it in detail in February 1943. Again, the Red Army learned from this crushing defeat and resolved to build better, more cohesive, tank armies to lead the offensives of 1943–44. Thus, the Tatsinskaya Raid played a significant experimental role in the evolution of Soviet tank doctrine and its ability to conduct future war-winning Deep Operations.

The 306. Infanterie Division moved up to the front, past Tatsinskaya, in mixed march formations. When Badanov's raid struck Tatsinskaya, one-third of the division was still south of the airbase. (Ian Barter)

German supply troops unload fuel at a forward airfield. The raid significantly disrupted Heeresgruppe Don's logistics, as well as the Stalingrad airlift. (Ian Barter)

Few other countries were willing to try deep armoured raids similar to that launched against Tatsinskaya, even when they had the opportunity. In March 1945, the American General George S. Patton conducted the unauthorized Hammelburg raid with Task Force Baum (314 men and 16 tanks) sent 80km (50 miles) behind German lines to rescue American prisoners of war. The results were very similar to the Tatsinskaya Raid: the raiders reached their objective but were encircled and destroyed by counter-attacking German forces, with only 11 per cent of the raiders returning to American lines. Together, the Tatsinskaya and Hammelburg raids indicate an interesting point about tanks in World War II – other than the mechanically reliable T-34 and Sherman tanks, there were few other tanks of that era that had the reliability and mobility to conduct raids deep behind enemy lines. Instead, most tanks of the era were still tied to infantry support roles and could not be expected to operate detached from their support elements for any length of time.

The actual loss of 46 transport aircraft at Tatsinskaya was painful for the Luftwaffe, but the Soviet Air Force had already destroyed at least 50 Ju-52 transports involved in the airlift to Stalingrad prior to Badanov's raid. Approximately 250 Luftwaffe transports involved in the airlift were lost either to enemy action, weather or mechanical malfunction in November–December 1942, of which the number lost at Tatsinskaya represents about one-fifth of the total. Rather than the loss of the aircraft, it was the loss of Tatsinskaya and the evacuation of Morozovskaya shortly thereafter that broke the back of the already inadequate Fliegerkorps VIII airlift operation.

For the Germans, their ability to save two-thirds of their transport aircraft from the Soviet raid and then crush the raiding force proved to be hollow triumphs. The efforts by Fliegerkorps VIII to conduct the airlift from other more distant airfields such as Salsk resulted in a greatly reduced flow of supplies into Stalingrad. Many of the transport planes saved at Tatsinskaya were shot down by the VVS over the next three weeks. Badanov's attempts to push on towards Morozovskaya actually assisted the German XXXXVIII Panzerkorps' counter-measures against the raid, since the raiding force was rushing towards the 11. Panzer-Division, rather than trying to evade a counter-attack. By the time that the 11. Panzer-Division engaged the 24th Tank Corps, the Soviet formation was reduced to fighting as individual battalions and brigades, which were defeated in detail. Indeed, the 11. Panzer-Division suffered only 15 killed and 74 wounded in its five-day effort to retake Tatsinskaya airfield and smash the 24th Tank Corps – surely a cheap, if somewhat unsatisfying victory.

Although XXXXVIII Panzerkorps succeeded in crushing the 24th Tank Corps at Tatsinskaya and temporarily saving Morozovskaya, the Soviet raid distracted this formation from its primary role of maintaining the defence of the Chir River line. Von Manstein was forced to divert his attention at a critical moment from the eastern flank of Heeresgruppe Don – where the fate of AOK 6 was being decided – to the western flank. Operation *Little Saturn* and the Tatsinskaya raid had placed von Manstein on the horns of a dilemma – should he commit his only remaining Panzer reserves to assist the now-hopeless effort to rescue AOK 6, or should he use it to preserve Heeresgruppe Don's own threatened lines of communication? Manstein chose the latter. Despite winning a tactical victory at Tatsinskaya, Heeresgruppe Don soon found itself in retreat virtually everywhere. With the failure of both the ground relief operation and the aerial resupply effort, AOK 6 was gradually smashed under relentless Soviet blows and its emaciated survivors finally surrendered on 2 February 1943.

CONCLUSION

The Red Army conducted a bold and unprecedented mechanized Deep Operation against Heeresgruppe Don's lines of communications and vital Luftwaffe air bases in December 1942, and achieved a partial success with strategic results. Although the sacrifice of two tank corps with almost 10,000 troops and 300 tanks in order to destroy 60 transport planes seems an extravagant price to pay, the raid did disrupt the airlift to Stalingrad and contributed to the surrender of AOK 6 and the retreat of Heeresgruppe Don. The appearance of such large Soviet tank units deep behind German lines had a profound effect on the morale of all Axis troops in Heeresgruppe Don and helped to solidify the gains made by Operations *Uranus* and *Little Saturn*.

Tactically, the raid demonstrated the limits of extended operations by mechanized units. By the time that Badanov reached his objective, his troops were exhausted and his tanks low on fuel and ammunition. Pavlov's corps staggered to a halt just short of its objective and Badanov's corps was combat ineffective soon after reaching its objective. Yet with a bit better coordination between ground and air units, Vatutin could have seized both objectives and recovered enough of his raiding forces to enable follow-on operations towards Rostov.

The lessons learned from the experience of Badanov's and Pavlov's tank corps helped to accelerate the Red Army's transition to the next logical phase of mechanized Deep Operations – the creation of tank armies. After World War II, the Soviet Army remained wedded to Isserson's original concept of Deep Operations, despite the advent of nuclear weapons, and it continued to hone the ideal raiding force into the Operational Manoeuvre Group (OMG). Developed in the 1950s and continuously updated until the fall of the Soviet Union, OMGs were postulated as independent mechanized groups ranging in size from several divisions up to a tank army. The concept was that after NATO lines were broken in an invasion of West Germany, the OMGs would penetrate deep into the enemy rear areas to overrun critical airfields such as Rhein Main airbase, where US reinforcements were expected to arrive. Fortunately, the end of the Cold War in the 1980s prevented this

The encircled 6. Armee finally surrendered six weeks after the Tatsinskaya raid. The disruption caused to the Luftwaffe airlift by the raid, as well as the failure of *Wintergewitter*, doomed any hope for even part of 6. Armee escaping or surviving until the spring. (Bundesarchiv, Bild 183-EO406-0022-010)

replay of the Tatsinskaya raid on a far grander scale.

After the war, the Tatsinskaya raid assumed a mythic quality in Soviet historiography about the Great Patriotic War, much of which was distorted. Despite the fact that the raid had accomplished its objective, many retired Soviet officers, including Zhukov and Badanov, felt compelled to lie about the results. In Zhukov's memoirs, he falsely claimed that the raid destroyed 300 German aircraft and that not a single Luftwaffe transport escaped. Badanov's account was particularly plagued with exaggeration, claiming that his corps had destroyed 431 German aircraft (more than the entire number involved in the Stalingrad airlift), 84 tanks (more than deployed by 6. and 11. Panzer-Divisionen against him) and captured or killed 11,292 enemy personnel. Yet most Soviet accounts shied away from mentioning Stalin's refusal to authorize Badanov to withdraw from the objective, which led to the virtual destruction of the 24th Tank Corps, and the faulty air–ground coordination that left Badanov's troops out on a limb. Soviet histories emphasized the positive aspects of the raid, but glossed over the fact that 72 per cent of the Fliegerkorps VIII transport force was able to escape. Most of all, Soviet accounts ignored Isserson's contribution to Deep Operations theory, and how it served as a vital doctrinal model for this unprecedented operation.

BIBLIOGRAPHY

Primary Records at National Archives and Records Administration (NARA), USA

Heeresgruppe Don, Ia Reports 15 December 1942–3 January 1943, T311, Rolls 269–270

11. Panzer-Division, Ic and IIa Reports, November–December 1942, T315, Roll 596

306. Infanterie-Division, Kriegstagbuch, November–December 1942, T315

Secondary Sources

Badanov, Vasily M., *Glubokii tankovyi reid* [Deep Tank Raid] in A.M. Samsonov (ed.) *Stalingradskaya epopeya*, Moscow, Nauka Publishers (1968), pp.625–40

Bekker, Cajus, *The Luftwaffe War Diaries*, New York, Ballantine Books (1966)

Bergström, Christer, *Stalingrad: The Air Battle 1942 through January 1943*, Hersham, Ian Allan Publishing (2007)

Glantz, David M., *From the Don to the Dnepr*, London, Frank Cass Publishers (1991)

Glantz, David M., *Soviet Operational Art Since 1936*

Kurowski, Franz, *Luftbrücke Stalingrad. Die Tragödie der Luftwaffe und der 6. Armee*

Vasil'ev, H. I., *Tatsinskii reid* [The Tatsinskaya Raid], Moscow, Voenizdat (1969)

Zhukov, Georgy K., *The Memoirs of Marshal Zhukov*, London, Jonathan Cape (1971)

INDEX